How to Meditate

A Step-by-Step Guide to the Art and Science of Meditation

D1487160

How to Meditate

A Step-by-Step Guide to the Art and Science of Meditation

Jyotish Novak

Revised Edition

Crystal Clarity Publishers
Nevada City, California

Crystal Clarity Publishers, Nevada City, CA 95959
Copyright © 2008, 1989 by John Novak
All rights reserved. Published 2008
First edition 1989. First edition revision 1992. Second edition 2008

ISBN13: 978-1-56589-234-7
Printed in U.S.A.
1 3 5 7 9 10 8 6 4 2

Cover photographs by Jyotish Novak, Barbara Bingham, Renee Glenn
Cover design by Renee Glenn Design
Interior design by Crystal Clarity Publishers

Library of Congress Cataloging-in-Publication Data
Novak, John (John Jyotish)
  How to meditate : a step-by-step guide to the art and science of meditation /
Jyotish Novak. — Rev. ed.
      p. cm.
  ISBN 978-1-56589-234-7 (trade paper)
  1. Meditation. I. Title.
  BL627.N68 2008
  204'.35—dc22
                                        2008024018

W: www.crystalclarity.com
E: clarity@crystalclarity.com
P: 800.424.1055

Contents

INTRODUCTION

This book was written to accompany "How to Meditate" classes I taught during the 1980's. I noticed that many students were engrossed in taking notes but were overlooking the essence of the course—the practice of the techniques. Meditation, you see, is learned by *doing* rather than by studying.

It became clear that those students would be greatly helped by a simple book that summarized the scope of what they were learning. This book is an effort to do just that. It covers all the material that was taught in those courses and gives the reader everything needed to start a practice of daily meditation.

Over the years since its first printing there has been an explosion in the numbers of meditators in Western countries, and now there are many millions who have a practice of daily meditation. According to the National Institutes of Health (NIH) survey, about 12% of U.S. adults use deep breathing exercises and 8% practice meditation. As the popularity of meditation has increased, there has been a growing demand for a short, practical guide that stays true to the ancient heritage of the art and science of meditation.

The material covered here is based primarily on the teachings of Paramhansa Yogananda and his disciple Swami Kriyananda, who is my teacher. Paramhansa Yogananda was one of the greatest yogis ever to teach in America. Coming to this country from India in 1920, he spent the next 32 years in the West writing books, lecturing to hundreds of thousands of students, and training dedicated disciples. He took the deepest philosophy and the highest techniques of the ancient science of Raja Yoga and put them into a language and system uniquely suited to the modern Western mind. His book, *Autobiography of a Yogi*, is a spiritual classic that has inspired innumerable readers throughout the world. More than 50 years after its first publishing, it continues to be on bestseller lists, having sold millions of copies.

Swami Kriyananda became Yogananda's disciple in 1948 and lived with him until the great master's passing in 1952. Kriyananda has taught yoga and its practical applications for over sixty years. At last count, he has written nearly one hundred books on the subject, including *The Path—My Life with Paramhansa Yogananda, One Man's Search on the Only Path There Is*, which tells about his years with Paramhansa Yogananda. Serious students naturally will want to supplement their practice of meditation with an understanding of the philosophy of life from which it springs. I cannot recommend highly enough the writings of these two great teachers.

Many of their major works are listed in the *Further Explorations* section at the end of this book.

In 1967 I became a student of Swami Kriyananda, and began teaching meditation a year later. In 1968 Kriyananda founded Ananda Village, a spiritual community based on the teachings of Paramhansa Yogananda, and located in the foothills of the Sierra Nevada Mountains of California. Ananda Village operates its own school system, businesses, and Meditation Retreat. Over the years Ananda has expanded to include residential communities and meditation centers in America, Europe, and India. Commonly considered one of the most successful examples of yogic living in the world, Ananda has nearly one thousand full-time residents overall, as well as over one hundred meditation groups and centers. The Ananda lifestyle is based on the daily practice of meditation, and, as Yogananda put it, "Plain living and high thinking." Ananda communities serve as a kind of living laboratory to test the benefits of these teachings.

For more information about Ananda, go to **www.ananda.org**. Knowing that a picture is worth a thousand words, we have also created a special *How to Meditate* website with free video and audio downloads of some of the material described in this book.

I am a founding member of Ananda, where I have lived and taught since 1969. My wife, Devi, and I serve as the Spiritual Directors of Ananda Worldwide. Over the last forty years I have had the opportunity to teach, counsel, and develop deep friendships with many hundreds of truth seekers. I have seen, first hand, the power of meditation to transform lives.

I pray that this book can serve as a guide to this wonderful science. May your quest be filled with joy.

Jyotish Novak

OVERVIEW OF MEDITATION

Chapter 1

Meditation is one of the most natural and most rewarding of all human activities. The great master of yoga, Paramhansa Yogananda, defined meditation as "deep concentration on God or one of His aspects." Practiced on a daily basis it produces astonishing results on all levels of your being: physical, mental, emotional, and spiritual. It connects you with your own inner powers of vitality, clarity, and love. When done deeply, it also gives you an expanded sense of connection with life and an experience of profound joy.

Meditation has three aspects: relaxation, interiorization, and expansion. The process, stated simply, is: a) Relax completely, both physically and mentally; b) Interiorize your mind and concentrate one-pointedly, usually at the point between the eyebrows; c) Focus your concentrated mind on an aspect of your own deeper self or of God, such as love, joy, or light. This will help to naturally expand your consciousness.

Although this process is simple to explain, the actual attainment of deeper states requires dedication and discipline. Yet even a little practice of meditation gives immediate results. Meditators find that practicing even a few minutes a day increases their sense of well-being and brings increased joy.

There is an innate yearning in each of us to expand our awareness, to know who and what we really are, and to experience union with God. At a certain stage in this "eternal quest," as Paramhansa Yogananda called it, we are guided to find inner stillness through the practice of meditation. Restless thoughts are a kind of mental "static" that must be silenced if we are to hear the whispers of our own inner self.

Profound perceptions about the nature of reality come through intuition rather than logic, from the superconscious rather than the conscious mind. When the body is completely relaxed, the five senses internalized, and the mind totally focused, a tremendous flow of energy becomes available. That intense energy can lift us into superconsciousness, where our inner powers of intuition are fully awake. Deep meditation helps us become aware of personal and universal realities barely dreamed of before, while even a little internalization of the consciousness lifts us *toward* that state and brings great peace.

Physiologically, meditation has been found, among other things, to reduce stress, strengthen the immune system, and help regulate many of the body's systems. During meditation the breath slows, blood pressure and metabolic rates decrease, and circulation and detoxification of the blood increase. Recent studies of patients with coronary artery disease showed that a combination of meditation, hatha yoga, and a natural vegetarian diet reverses heart disease far better than the best medical treatment presently available. Meditation changes the frequency and intensity of brain waves in beneficial ways and has even been shown to increase the size of the frontal lobes of the brain.

Mentally, meditation focuses and clarifies the mind. James J. Lynn, the most advanced disciple of Paramhansa Yogananda, was the founder and chief executive of one of the largest insurance companies in America. He often arrived at his office late in the morning after several hours of meditation. When associates asked how he could accomplish all his work with such a "relaxed" schedule, he responded that meditation enabled him to do his work much more efficiently. With his mind completely centered, he was able to make decisions in a few moments that otherwise might have taken weeks.

While the physical and mental benefits of meditation are great, it is first and foremost a spiritual art. Its purpose, ultimately, is to lead us to perfection, to the realization that we are one with the Infinite. We come from God and are made in His image, and our hearts are restless until we achieve unity (*yoga* in Sanskrit) with Him again. Like lotuses opening to the sun, we are compelled by our own higher nature, the spark of God within, to experience increasingly expanded states of awareness. Meditation is the direct pathway to this unified state.

In recent years meditation has become widely accepted and practiced in the West. It is now taught in churches, recommended by physicians, and widely practiced by athletes. There are meditation chapels in airports, hospitals, and even in Congress.

It is an ancient art, going back in time to a period long before historical records were kept. Stone seals showing people seated in various yoga postures have been found in the Indus Valley of India, and have been dated by archaeologists as far back as 5000 B.C. Yet meditation is much more than an interesting but long-forgotten ancient practice. For many thousands of years, it has remained a dynamic discipline, renewed again and again by the experiences of saints and sages of all religions.

Every religion has some branch (often somewhat secret) that seeks mystical union, with its own form of meditation to achieve that end. Every age has examples of great men and women who have achieved Self-realization, or union with the Divine. The East, especially India, has developed the science and tradition of meditation. Over the centuries great sages and teachers discovered truths and techniques, which they passed on to their disciples, who in turn passed them on to their followers. Generation followed generation in an unbroken tradition for thousands of years. This tradition continually refreshed the practices—those which proved true and lasting survived, while those which were tainted with ignorance fell by the wayside. Moreover, the East developed a culture that looked to enlightened beings as examples of how to live. In India, children are still taught through stories and examples from the lives of Self-realized souls such as Rama and Krishna, two great saints of ancient India. It has been said that the greatness of a culture can be judged by its heroes. In the East, and particularly in India, the greatest heroes have been those of the highest spiritual attainments.

The West, however, has lacked a living tradition of meditation passed on from master to disciple. Great saints there have certainly been, but usually they have been self-taught men and women who had to discover the pathway to mystical union with little or no outside help. Moreover, they often knew no techniques to channel the enormous inner energy awakened by their intense devotion. Without teachers to guide them, or techniques to help them, their inner energies became obstructed, and many were beset with great physical suffering. In a society that didn't understand or necessarily respect sanctity, many had to face the opposition of their families and even their spiritual "superiors."

In the West our heroes have tended to be more warlike than Godlike. Mahatma Gandhi was once asked what he thought of Western civilization. His wry but charming reply was, "I think it would be a good idea."

Finally, with the inflow of teachings from India, the tradition and benefits of meditation are being introduced to the West, and a new tradition is developing. The practice of meditation has tremendous potential for enriching both our individual lives and our society. The historian Arnold Toynbee has called the introduction of the Eastern spiritual traditions into the West the most important influence in the twentieth century.

GETTING STARTED

Chapter 2

Meditation can be done virtually any time and anywhere that you can find a little peace and quiet. All you really need is space to disconnect from outward activity and concentrate on inner realities. As a beginner you can start with as little as 15 to 20 minutes a day. However, as you begin to experience the benefits of meditation, you will probably want to increase the amount of time.

Meditation is not dependent upon belief or dogma, but is, like science, based on experimentation and experience. Just as science seeks to explore the physical world, meditation seeks to probe the world of consciousness itself. Its tools, rather than microscopes and oscilloscopes, are concentration and intuition, and its discoveries are verifiable. In science an experiment is accepted after other qualified scientists are able to reproduce the results. The same is true for the subtle perceptions and insights gained in meditation.

Countless adepts of meditation have repeatedly verified them throughout the ages.

Meditation requires only a willing heart and an inquiring mind, but here are a few helpful aids that can make the practice easier.

Set Aside a Special Area for Meditation

It is very helpful to have an area that is used only for meditation, as it will help reinforce a state of interiorization and, over time, become filled with meditative "vibrations." A small room or closet is ideal as long as it can be well ventilated. If you don't have enough space to set aside an entire room for this, then find a small area in your bedroom or some other room that can be used just for meditation. This area can be very simple—all you really need is a small cushion or a chair to sit on.

Many people find it helpful to set up a small altar with pictures of great souls who inspire them. You may want to have a candle for evening meditations and perhaps an incense burner. Your altar can be elaborate or simple, according to your own tastes. It can include anything that will help you to both concentrate and uplift your consciousness.

The meditation room that my wife and I use is about the size of a walk-in closet. There is a bench which is covered with a woolen pad, wide enough on which to sit cross-legged or that can be used like a chair. Our altar includes the pictures of our line of gurus, a pair of candles, and a few objects that are sacred to us.

You can meditate in any quiet spot, if you have no area that can be set aside. The true altar is, in any case, a pure heart.

Cooperate with Natural Forces

There are certain natural forces that can either help or oppose your efforts. Magnetic forces in the earth tend to pull one's energy down. Certain natural fibers serve as insulation against these forces just as a coating of rubber insulates an electrical wire. Traditionally, yogis sat on the skin of a tiger or deer that had died a natural death. Since these are rather hard to find these days, it works nearly as well to cover your meditation seat with a woolen blanket, a silk cloth, or both.

Especially good times to meditate are dawn, dusk, noon, and midnight. At these times, the gravitational pull of the sun works in harmony with the natural polarities of the body. It is somewhat easier to meditate at night or early in the morning while others are asleep. Thoughts have power, and the restless thoughts of people around you will have a subtle tendency to make your meditations more restless. For many years, when my wife and I were the leaders of an ashram in San Francisco, we held our group meditations quite early in the morning. As the sun rose and the city started to come awake, we could easily feel the increasing restlessness of our neighborhood.

Develop Good Habits

Developing good habits will be *the most important factor* in determining whether or not you succeed in establishing a practice of meditation. Good intentions and bursts of enthusiastic devotion will dissipate unless they become translated into daily routine.

The first thing to do is decide on *when* is the most convenient time for you to meditate. In choosing a time, regularity is the most important factor, so set a time when you can be consistent. Meditate every day at your chosen time, even if you meditate for only five or ten minutes at a time. If, for at least 30 days, you make a consistent effort never to skip a meditation, a supportive habit will start to form, and it will become easier.

Try to meditate fifteen to twenty minutes twice a day in the beginning, and then increase the time gradually, but don't push yourself beyond your capacity to enjoy meditation. As you progress you will find that you naturally want to meditate longer. The more you meditate, the more you will enjoy it! Once you have established a routine, stick with it until a strong habit is formed. If time is short, remember, the depth of a meditation is more important than the length.

For most people, the best times to meditate are just after rising in the morning and before going to bed at night. These times are the least likely to have scheduling conflicts or competing demands. It is also easier to re-program the subconscious mind, where habits are rooted, just after or before sleep. Many people also like to meditate before lunch or after work before eating dinner. If you meditate after a meal, it is best to wait at least one half hour, and up to three hours after a heavy meal, so there will not be competition for energy between meditation and digestion.

A very helpful means of increasing the length and depth of your meditations is to have at least one longer meditation each week. Your long meditation should be about two or three times as long as your normal ones. If you are normally meditating for twenty minutes at a sitting, try to meditate once a week for an hour. Not only will you find that you can go deeper in the long meditation, but your usual twenty minutes will soon begin to seem short.

Group meditation is also very helpful. If possible, try to join a group of people who meditate regularly. The encouragement of others who have been meditating longer than you is a very powerful spiritual force. Ananda has many meditation groups around the country, which can be found on our website, **www.ananda.org**

There are three stages to meditation: relaxation, concentration, and expansion. Each one is important and none can be neglected, especially if you want to achieve the deeper states that are possible. Fortunately there are a variety of strategies and techniques to accomplish in each stage.

Key Points

Getting Started

❖ Place a woolen blanket, silk cloth, or both on your seat.

❖ Develop a regular habit, meditating 15–20 minutes daily at the same time each day. Twice a day is even better.

❖ Set aside a special area for meditation to build the power.

❖ Try one longer meditation each week.

STAGE ONE — RELAXATION

The biggest challenge in meditation is to concentrate the mind. Even experienced meditators have difficulty with this, and must strive to overcome whatever distractions are preventing them from concentrating. The first thing that must be dealt with is physical tension. When the body moves or is tense, the motor nerves send signals to the brain that disrupt concentration. Fortunately, given a little attention, it is quite easy to achieve a sufficiently relaxed physical state. More challenging will be mental relaxation, but we'll discuss that later.

To some extent the chronic tension and restlessness of both body and mind is simply a result of habit. We are used to moving and tensing, planning and worrying. Gradually, habitual tension becomes so deeply entrenched that it feels abnormal to let the body relax and the mind become quiet. In fact, much of modern culture, especially advertising, is designed to keep us in a state of desire and anxiety. It takes some effort of will to overcome the influences of culture and habit.

As you sit to meditate, it is very important to make a strong mental resolution to put aside all preoccupations and worries. Be determined to withdraw from all involvement for a little while. Your problems and worries will still be there when you return. Christ said it beautifully: "Seek ye first the kingdom of God, and His righteousness; and all these things shall be added unto you. Take therefore no thought for the morrow: for the morrow shall take thought for the things of itself. Sufficient unto the day is the evil thereof." (Matthew 6:33,34)

There is a charming story from India of a man who was taking his ritual bath in the Ganges. A holy man asked him why he was doing it, to which the man replied, "Well, you see, bathing in the Ganges washes off all my sins." The holy man said with a chuckle, "That may be true, but they wait for you in the trees and jump on you when you come out again."

There is actually a deeper meaning to this story. The Ganges is used as a symbol of the river of *prana* or life-force that flows in the inner spine. Immersing one's consciousness in that stream of intuitive energy helps wash away worries, ignorance, and pre-occupations. But, like that poor man's sins, they usually wait for you to end your meditation and jump on you again.

The first step in meditation is physical relaxation.

Relaxing the Body

Chapter 3

The ability to relax the body at will is the vital first step for meditation, but this skill also has benefits for every aspect of life. There is a feedback loop between the body and the mind—a complex cascade of signals exchanged between muscles and brain. If the body is tense or restless, the mind will follow, and vice versa. Just observe the tension in your muscles the next time you are about to have a difficult meeting. We can use this feedback loop to our advantage—by relaxing physically, we will automatically start to relax mentally.

It is very helpful to do a couple of simple relaxation techniques before actually starting meditation. Here are two easy yoga postures that will help prepare both the body and mind.

Deep Yogic Breath

Begin by standing upright, arms at the sides. Relax completely and center your consciousness in the spine, visualizing it as the trunk of a tall tree. Become aware of your breath, and watch to see that you are breathing deeply from the diaphragm.

Now slowly bend forward, keeping the knees relaxed. Exhale slowly and completely as you bend forward, allowing your body to come down only as far as is comfortable and your hands to relax toward your feet. Pause and relax for a few seconds in this position. Now inhale slowly as you raise the torso. As the inhalation continues and your body slowly comes upright, draw the hands up along the sides of the body, elbows extended outward. With the incoming breath, feel that you are drawing not only air, but also energy and life-force, into every cell of the body and brain. Continue inhaling and raising the trunk and arms, finally stretching the hands high above the head. At this point you should have inhaled as completely as possible. Hold this position for a few seconds. Now slowly exhale and relax into the forward bend again. Repeat this three or four times. End by exhaling into the original standing position with the arms at the sides. *(See illustration of the Deep Yogic Breath on page 29.)*

The Corpse Pose (Savasana)

This posture is called the Corpse Pose because it helps withdraw all tension from the muscles. It is both the simplest and yet one of the most difficult of all the yoga postures. Physically it is extremely easy. The difficulty is that to practice it to perfection one must relax totally—not an easy thing for most people.

Lie flat on your back with your legs extended, feet slightly apart, and your arms along the sides of your body. The body should be properly aligned, with the head, neck, trunk, and legs in a straight line. It is best to have the palms turned upward to help to induce a feeling of receptivity.

After assuming this position, begin a systematic relaxation of the whole body. Start by ridding the body of unconscious tension: first, tense the body to increase the tension and then relax completely. There is a special "double breath" which helps oxygenate the system and remove toxins. It is done by inhaling through the nose with a short inhalation followed immediately by a longer one, in a huh/ huuuuhh rhythm. The exhalation with a double breath is through both the nose and mouth with the same short/long rhythm.

Inhale deeply with a double breath, tense the whole body until it vibrates, then throw the breath out in a double exhalation and relax the body by releasing the tension. Stay relaxed for a few seconds and then do this again, three to six times, trying to relax your whole body after each round.

Deep Yogic Breath

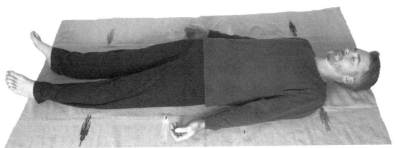

The Corpse Pose

Now, consciously do a deep relaxation of the various body parts, starting with the feet. It may help to think of the area being relaxed as filling with space and growing very light, or conversely, so relaxed that it is extremely heavy and impossible to move. Gradually work your way up the body, relaxing successively the calves, knees (especially behind the knees, a common area of subconscious tension), thighs, hips, abdomen (another common trouble spot), hands, forearms, upper arms, chest, neck, and face. As you get to the head, be sure to focus on relaxing the jaw and tongue, the areas around the eyes, and the forehead. When you have relaxed the whole body, continue to lie still, resting in this deeply relaxed state for several minutes.

To deepen your relaxation even further, you can feel that you are floating on a warm sea and your breathing is matching the rhythm of the rise and fall of the waves. Let go of every vestige of tension as you become deeply relaxed both physically and mentally. Feel that you are melting into the sea, becoming one with it and with all life. Try to hold on to this relaxed, expanded state for several minutes, and try not to let your mind wander during this process. If you find yourself daydreaming, bring your awareness back to the here and now, being aware of your breathing and your deeply relaxed state.

When it feels right to do so, gradually let your energy return to the body. Sit up slowly, staying as relaxed as possible, and go directly into your meditation.

Diaphragmatic Breathing

The deep relaxation of the corpse pose can also help you learn to breathe properly. Proper breathing starts with the diaphragm, a dome shaped sheet of muscle dividing the abdomen from the chest cavity. As this muscle contracts, it pushes down into the abdominal cavity, creating a space above it so the lungs can expand and draw in oxygen. A secondary expansion of the lungs is produced by expanding the rib cage and the chest. Deep, diaphragmatic breathing oxygenates and energizes the whole system. Unfortunately, few of us breathe properly.

A perfect time to practice diaphragmatic breathing is during the corpse pose, when you are already deeply relaxed. As you breathe, allow the relaxed abdomen to expand gently upward with the inhalation and downward with the exhalation, which some people call "breathing like a baby." In the beginning you may want to exaggerate this movement in order to help retrain yourself. After

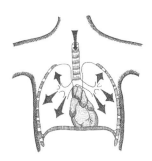 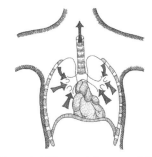

Expanded Chest and Contracted Chest

finishing the corpse pose, stand upright for a while, and continue to practice diaphragmatic breathing in an upright position.

Proper breathing also depends on proper posture. If you slump, it compresses the abdomen so the diaphragm doesn't have the space to expand. Train yourself to stand and sit with the chest up, the shoulders slightly back, and the spine straight. This position not only helps you breathe properly but also allows your body to relax more completely when you meditate.

A straight spine is important for spiritual reasons also. Many of the more advanced techniques of yoga work with energies in the subtle, or *astral* spine. A tremendous storehouse of energy, the *Kundalini* power, normally remains coiled at the base of the spine. By concentrating at the point between the eyebrows or by using other techniques, we can help this energy to rise in the subtle spine so that enlightenment can take place.

In India there is even a special order of swamis, called *Danda Swamis*, who carry a bamboo staff to remind themselves to always keep the spine straight. Learn to live more "in the spine," centered in the inner self, rather than reacting constantly to the events and worries of the world.

Proper Posture for Meditation

In order to be able to relax the body sufficiently for meditation, proper posture is very important. And yet, there is nothing complicated about it. Simply sit upright with the spine erect and the body relaxed. The chest should be up, the shoulders slightly back, and the chin parallel to the floor. Imagine yourself as a marionette with a string pulling you upright from the top of the skull, allowing everything to fall into place. This position allows the spine to bear the weight of the torso, whereas a bent spine requires muscular tension to counteract the unbalanced forces.

You can sit either in a straight-backed chair or on the floor in a comfortable cross-legged pose. If you are flexible, you will probably find it easier to sit on the floor. The traditional posture for meditation is the lotus pose, which locks the body into an upright posture, but any comfortable position is fine. If you sit on the floor, you will probably find a small cushion under the buttocks helpful. Sit straight with the shoulders back, slightly corrugating the upper back, and the hands, palms upright, at either the junction of the thighs and trunk, or resting on the knees.

If you prefer a chair, use one that is not too soft and that allows you to keep your spine upright. Sit forward so nothing presses against your back. Place the hands, palms upright, at the junction of the thighs and abdomen to help keep the spine erect and the chest open. Your feet should rest flat on the floor. As mentioned earlier, whether you sit on a chair or on the floor, it is helpful to cover your meditation seat with a woolen blanket, a silk cloth, or both.

As you sit to meditate, first be sure the body is relaxed. If you have just finished the corpse pose, a quick mental check to see that you are still relaxed should be sufficient. If you have not yet relaxed the body, you can do so as soon as you begin. Follow the same routine as in preparing for the Corpse Pose, *Savasana*. First inhale with a double breath, tense the whole body until it vibrates, then throw the breath out with a double breath. Do this three to six times. Then starting with the feet, work your way up the body to the head, consciously relaxing every body part. When you are completely relaxed physically, it is time to relax mentally.

Cross-legged Posture for Meditation

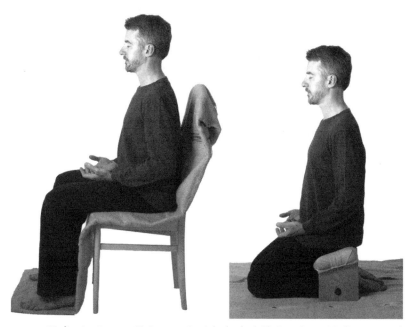

Meditation Posture: Sitting on a Straight-backed Chair and on a Meditation Bench

Key Points

Relaxing the Body

➤ Do a few minutes of physical relaxation before sitting, using the Deep Yogic Breath or the Corpse Pose.

➤ Learn and practice proper diaphragmatic breathing.

➤ Sit with a relaxed but upright spine. You can sit either on the floor or in a chair.

➤ As a preparation for meditation, be sure to deeply relax the various body parts, starting with the feet and working up to the forehead.

RELAXING THE MIND
Chapter 4

Just as it is necessary to release tensions in the muscles, it is also essential to relax any tension in the mind. Mental tension is caused primarily by worries—either preoccupations about the past or anxieties and desires about the future. If we could remain completely in the here and now, it would be easy to stay relaxed and happy.

There was a time in my life when I was starting an incense business for Ananda, our spiritual community. It was an intense time, as any entrepreneur can attest, with long hours, little money, and countless details vying for my attention. I found it very difficult to calm my mind and stay focused in the here and now. A thousand little thoughts kept calling out, "What about me? I'm important." Worries seemed to be my main mental diet. One day as I sat trying to meditate, an image came powerfully into my mind, "Time is like a river and you are floating in it. You can never occupy more than one place in any given moment, so focus on where you are right now, and let the rest of the river take care of itself." Somehow, that image had the power to help me focus. Whenever I found my mind wandering into worries or "to do" lists, I visualized a river, and it brought me back to my center.

Meditation will help produce a more centered state, but we must relax, at least partially, before its effects will start. One of the most effective ways to relax the mind is to observe the breath. From ancient times, yogis have recognized the direct link between the breath and the mind. In fact, the science of controlling the mind through breathing techniques, called *pranayama*, is one of India's great gifts to the world.

The word *prana* has three meanings: energy, life, and breath. *Prana* is used, first of all, to describe the universal sea of energy that infuses and vitalizes all matter. This sea of energy coalesces into sub-atomic particles and atoms, which become the basic building blocks of all matter manifesting the physical world. So, every atom, molecule, and cell is an extension of prana, just as waves are extensions of the sea that lies beneath them.

Secondly, *prana* is used to mean the vitalizing power that flows in all living forms and performs vital functions. Paramhansa Yogananda called this aspect of prana "life-force." He further explained that life-force possesses an inherent intelligence enabling it to carry out the life-sustaining processes. To give clarity to this image, he even coined the term "lifetrons."

We have a subtle or astral body made up of prana that underlies the physical body. Oriental healing techniques, such as Ayurveda and acupuncture, work to harmonize and strengthen the flow of life-force, calling it variously *prana, chi, or ki*. When the life-force flows properly, the result will be a natural state of health and vitality.

Finally, and very important to the science of yoga, *prana* is also used to refer to the breath. When we take a physical breath, there is a corresponding movement of prana in the subtle or astral spine. Prana flows up in the subtle spine in conjunction with the inhalation, and down with the exhalation. This link between breath and the flow of prana is central to many of the techniques of meditation. By controlling the breath, which is easily felt, we can influence the flow of prana, which is much more subtle and difficult to feel. Traditional *pranayama* (*prana* = energy + *yama* = control) techniques involve various ways of controlling the breathing.

A direct feedback cycle also exists between the flow of breath (prana) and the mind. A nervous or excited mental state is always accompanied by ragged breathing. You can help to calm the mind by first controlling the breath. You will notice that when you have a task requiring concentration, such as threading a needle, you automatically tend to slow or even hold your breath. The next time you are in a nervous frame of mind, try breathing your way out of it using the deep yogic breath or one of the simple exercises below. You can use breathing techniques even in times of great stress.

Mike, a friend and fellow disciple, was in charge of training new recruits for the San Francisco Police. One technique he taught the rookies was to control their breathing before trying to take control of a tense situation. "Take slow relaxed breaths," he told them, "in order to keep yourself calm and focused." He illustrated the importance of self-control through breath-control with this true story:

One time, during a drug raid, Mike chased a man up a stairway in a darkened building. As he got to the top of the stairs, he turned down a narrow hallway, and found the suspect pointing a shotgun at his chest. The man was obviously "high" on something, and Mike knew that one false move on his part could be fatal. While holding the man's eyes with his own, he immediately started breathing deeply, and mentally affirmed, "Be calm, be centered." After a few moments he slowly held out his hand and asked the man to give him the gun. The man's shoulders slumped as the tension went out of him, and he surrendered without violence.

In the Olympic biathlon the participants must combine the extreme outward effort needed for cross-country skiing with the fine concentration needed to hit a target with a rifle shot. Some years ago the sport was transformed when the power of breath control was discovered. Now, as the participants race the last few hundred yards toward the target sites, these world-class competitors use special techniques to control their breathing, which slows the heart and concentrates the mind.

Most of us won't have our mental control tested under such extreme conditions, but our meditations can benefit from the connection that exists between breath control and mind control. Here are a couple of simple breathing techniques that will relax the mind. The first one, "regular breathing," should be used at the beginning of every meditation.

Regular Breathing

Immediately after you have finished relaxing the various body parts, use this technique to relax the mind: Inhale slowly, counting to twelve. Hold the breath for the same number of counts while concentrating at the point between the eyebrows. Then slowly exhale for the same twelve counts. This is one round of "regular breathing." Do six to nine rounds as you start to meditate. You can increase the count to 16:16:16, or decrease the number of counts to 8:8:8, according to your capacity, but be sure that the three phases—inhalation, retention, and exhalation—are all equal. Generally speaking, a slower rhythm is better, providing you are comfortable and don't get out of breath. Especially in the later rounds, you may want to increase the number of counts.

Concentrate completely on the breath, feeling it flowing in and out like the tide. As you exhale, let go of all restless or negative thoughts. When you inhale, feel that you are filling yourself not only with air but also with calm vitality. If you find your mind has wandered, immediately bring it back by concentrating on the breath. Focus on the breath itself rather than the breathing process. These first few minutes of meditation are extremely important because they set the tone for the whole period. Start concentrating with the very first breath and it will help you stay focused throughout your whole meditation.

Regular breathing is such a simple but effective technique that it can be used in a variety of situations. The next time you become nervous, do a few rounds of regular breathing, and you will notice an immediate calming influence. You can rarely *think* yourself out of a negative or anxious state, but you can often *breathe* yourself out of one.

Alternate Breathing

There is another simple breathing exercise or *pranayam* that you will find helpful—"alternate breathing." This is similar to regular breathing, except that the breath is inhaled through one nostril and exhaled through the other. Close the right nostril with the thumb of the right hand and inhale through the left nostril for a count of twelve. Then hold the breath for the same count. During the retention phase, gently squeeze the nostrils shut, using the thumb for one nostril and the ring finger for the other. Hold the breath in this manner, concentrating deeply at the point between the eyebrows for twelve counts. Then, keeping the left nostril closed with the ring finger, exhale through the right nostril. In hatha yoga there are names given for each phase: *purak* for inhalation, *kumbhak* for retention, and *rechak* for exhalation.

As in regular breathing, you can vary the number of counts according to what is comfortable, but keep the same count for all three phases. This exercise is "cooling" to the nervous system and helps calm the mind because it works in harmony with the natural flows of magnetic energy in the body. Energy moves up the left side of the subtle spine as we inhale and down on the right as we exhale.

Alternate Breathing

You may want to experiment by doing a variation of this technique. Do one round as described above and then the next round inhaling through the right nostril and exhaling through the left. This reverses the natural flow and gives an entirely different feeling, which many find heating or energizing to the nervous system.

Especially good for concentration is a variation in which the inhalation and exhalation are the normal twelve counts each, but the breath is held for a longer period of time, up to 25 or more counts, during the retention phase. Concentrate with great determination at the point between the eyebrows (also called the spiritual eye) while holding your breath.

These simple techniques are more important than you might think. People can meditate for many months, or even years, with little results, simply because they have ignored the basics, thinking that such elementary practices are only for the merest beginner. Restlessness, especially mental restlessness, is the main impediment to deeper meditation, and these basic breathing exercises are extremely effective in stilling the thoughts. For one thing, they serve as a focal point for concentration, which breaks the momentum of mental tumult. But more importantly, these techniques work with subtle energies little understood in the West.

"Our thoughts," Yogananda said, "are universally, not individually rooted." The astounding ramifications of this statement reverse the present-day model of the thinking process. Instead of creating our own thoughts, we draw them from a universal pool of consciousness much as a radio receives a program. As we change the magnetism of our consciousness, we change the "station" we receive. Mental restlessness is like static that prevents the program from being heard clearly. Our hardest job in meditation is to rid the mind of the static created by thoughts and desires. As soon as we can do this, we will rise to a higher level of consciousness where we can see that our reality is not the ego (the receiver), but God, the Creator.

The reason that meditation is so important to a spiritual search is that it is designed specifically to calm the mind and rid it of the whirlpools (or static) of separative consciousness. Once we have removed the false boundaries and expanded the perception of "I am" to infinity, we will finally realize our true self. This is the state of the enlightened soul.

But, the journey of a thousand miles begins with a single step, and the first step is relaxation. Once the body and mind have been relaxed, we are ready to proceed to the second stage of meditation: concentration.

Key Points
Relaxing the Mind

➴ To relax the mind, use the breathing techniques of regular breathing or alternate breathing.

➴ These breathing techniques can be used any time you want to calm your mind or emotions.

➴ Focus deeply at the point between the eyebrows during the retention phase and also after finishing the technique.

STAGE TWO—CONCENTRATION & INTERIORIZATION

CONCENTRATION & INTERIORIZATION
Chapter 5

The next stage of meditation is concentration and the interiorization of energy which takes place on physical, mental, and more subtle planes. In his book *Affirmations for Self-Healing*, Swami Kriyananda writes:

> "Concentration is the secret of success in every undertaking. Without concentration, thoughts, energy, inspiration, purpose—all one's inner forces—become scattered. Concentration is the calm focus of one's full attention on the purpose at hand. Concentration means more than mental effort: It means channeling your heart's feelings, your faith, and your deep aspirations into whatever you are doing. In that way, even the little things in life can become rich with meaning.
>
> Concentration should not involve mental strain. When you really want something, it is difficult *not* to think about it! Concentrate *with interest* on whatever you do, and you will find yourself absorbed in it."

While concentration is helpful for success in any area, it is absolutely essential for meditation, which by definition, requires deep concentration. A special type of attention is needed in meditation, where the mind is focused on inward realities rather than external objects. When we engage in outward activity, our thoughts are normally focused on the object of our attention: a person, a book, the eye of a needle. But in order to carry on our inner search we need to withdraw our attention from the things of the world and focus on a more inward reality such as the breath, or light seen in the forehead.

In meditation all of our scattered forces must be brought to a single point of concentration, usually at the spiritual eye, which is located at the point between the eyebrows in the frontal part of the brain. This is the center of will and intuition, and the seat of superconsciousness or total awareness. Enlightenment takes place when all energy (or prana) is focused at this point. This center is also associated with feelings of joy. Recent studies involving brain imaging show that when this center is more active, the participants report feeling happy, alert, and even blissful. Long-time meditators, even when they are not meditating, have more activity in this prefrontal section of the brain and less in those centers that are associated with fear, anxiety, and negative emotions.

There are other states of consciousness, other than meditation, when our energy is inwardly focused. Every night in sleep, energy is withdrawn from the senses and muscles and refocused in the brain. Many sleepers are completely lost to the world. In fact, this interiorization of energy and attention is the primary reason that sleep is refreshing. As far as the withdrawal of energy is concerned, sleep and meditation are similar. But in sleep we are unaware, while in deep meditation we are more than normally alert, lifting our consciousness into a superconscious state. If we could have the physical and sensory immobilization of sleep but not lose consciousness we could, theoretically, make very rapid spiritual progress. Paramhansa Yogananda humorously referred to sleep as "counterfeit *samadhi.*"

The biggest threats to meditation are the restless thoughts and anxieties that ceaselessly play in the background of our mental screen. These are usually subdued when something engages our full attention, as when we become completely absorbed during an exciting movie. But, when we try to relax and focus inwardly, we often find it very difficult to shut off the mental static. Instead of calm focus, we tend to think about the past, worry and plan for the future, or daydream. However, with a strong intention to concentrate and the use of some helpful techniques, we can overcome these distractions.

There is a story of a greedy businessman who heard about a saint who was able to levitate. Thinking of how much he could save on travel expenses with such a power, the man went to learn from the saint. The yogi surprised the man by saying that levitation was quite simple and gave him a mantra to repeat during meditation. The greedy fellow, rubbing his hands in anticipation, was just about to leave, when the saint said, "Oh, just one more thing: it's very important that you don't think about monkeys while repeating this mantra." The man was puzzled, but not upset with this advice, since he never thought about monkeys anyway.

That evening, as he sat to meditate and repeat his mantra, he immediately remembered the caution about monkeys. Within minutes he was pondering the wide variety of different species of monkeys that he was not supposed to think about. Then he began to think about the amusing habits of monkeys. That night he dreamed about monkeys, and the next day found him at the library researching the subject. Finally, after a week of this, he returned to the saint and said, "You can have your mantra back. I don't want it. All it has done is to make me obsessed with monkeys." The yogi laughed and said, "You came here with monkey consciousness—all I did was to help you become aware of it." He then gave him some basic instruction so the man could gradually improve himself. The question of levitation never came up again.

There are a number of practices that help us concentrate and interiorize the mind. The relaxation and breathing techniques we have already learned will start the process. But yogis have developed more powerful techniques to help us focus mental energy. Three of the most powerful techniques are watching the breath, chanting (or repeating a mantra or prayer), and visualization.

Watching the Breath

Watching the breath is one of the central and most widely taught techniques of Raja Yoga. Although simple to practice, watching the breath is extremely powerful because it takes advantage of the breath-prana-mind cycle in a scientific manner. By concentrating intently on the breath and simply observing the inhalation and exhalation, we can influence prana to flow toward the spiritual eye. This, in turn, helps us to concentrate more deeply, by withdrawing energy that is otherwise directed outward through the senses. Here is the method:

1   The technique of watching the breath should be done immediately following the preparatory techniques that you've already learned. If possible, start by doing some of the techniques for relaxing the body. Then as you sit for meditation, make a conscious determination to focus your mind during the entire time of your meditation. Begin with a few rounds of regular or alternate breathing. Then inhale with a double breath, tense the whole body until it vibrates, throw the breath out with a double exhalation and relax deeply. Do this three to six times. Now starting with the feet, deeply relax the whole body, as you have already learned. Finally concentrate at the point between the eyebrows and release all mental tension.

2   After relaxing both the body and the mind, you need a focal point for concentration. This is the breath. Begin by taking a deep breath, and then do a triple exhalation to expel the air completely. As the next breath flows in and then out, mentally watch it as if you were observing the rise and fall of a swell on the sea. Be very aware of the inhalation and exhalation, but make no attempt to control them in any way. Simply observe their natural flow. Try physically to feel the breath as it passes in and out of the nostrils. If you are unable to feel the breath in the nostrils, focus for a short time on the breathing process itself, the movement of the chest and lungs, and then transfer your awareness back to the breath in the nostrils.

3   To help deepen your concentration you can use a powerful word formula, or mantra, called *"hong-sau."* This is what yogis call a *bija* mantra, where the sounds themselves have power even though they are not actually

words. Silently repeat "*hong*" (rhymes with "song") with the incoming breath and "*sau*" (sounds like "saw") with the exhalation. This particular mantra is especially effective for calming the flow of prana in the spine.

If you would prefer, you can mentally repeat a more familiar word such as "Amen" in conjunction with the breath. As you inhale, silently say "A," and as you exhale silently repeat "men." Or you could say "I am" while inhaling and "He" while exhaling, which is a rough translation of "hong-sau." Or simply count "one" with the incoming breath and "two" with the outgoing breath.

It is also helpful to move the index finger of the right hand slightly toward the palm on the inhalation and slightly away on the exhalation.

 If the mind wanders, immediately bring it back to concentrating on the breath. This is *very important*. The breath gives us a reference point, as it were. One of the problems with a wandering mind is that, without a reference point, we don't have an easy way to recognize that it has wandered. The breath gives us that point. Any thought or mental image other than observing the breath can now be recognized as being a distraction. As soon as you realize your mind has wandered, bring it back to the breath.

5   As the breath becomes calmer, gradually feel it higher and higher in the nostrils until you are watching it high up in the nasal cavity. It may take some minutes to get calm and centered enough to feel the breath there.

6   Now you can transfer your concentration from the flow of the breath to the point between the eyebrows. This area (called the "spiritual eye") is, according to the teachings of yoga, the center of will power. By concentrating at this point and keeping your attention from wandering, you gradually bring the flow of prana under the control of your will, enabling you to interiorize it. Try to go ever deeper until your mind is completely focused on observing the breath and silently repeating your word formula. Remember, make no effort to control either how fast or how deep you're breathing. Just let the breath naturally calm itself.

As your concentration begins to center at the point between the eyebrows, you will notice that your gaze (behind your closed eyelids) is also lifting upwards. The upward gaze follows the uplifted awareness. The angle of the eyes also *encourages* uplifted awareness. Therefore, you will find it helpful, from the beginning of your meditation, to lift your gaze slightly, behind the closed eyelids. This upward angle of the eyes should gentle and comfortable, as if you were looking at a mountain in the distance. If you feel any strain in the eyes or the forehead, you should lower the gaze slightly.

Gazing upward will take a little getting used to. Don't focus all of your attention on it, but work with it over time. It quickly becomes a habit, and you will notice that it helps your mind to stay focused.

7   The key to success with the "Hong-sau technique" is to deepen your concentration at the spiritual eye until you no longer think about *anything* except the rhythmic flow of the breath. As the mind becomes very calm, you will find your need to breathe diminishing. Enjoy the spaces

between breaths, keeping your mind very still and allowing the pauses to lengthen naturally. A cycle of increasing interiorization is set into motion through this technique. As the breath (and the flow of life-force) begins to calm down, the mind is naturally able to concentrate more deeply. Deeper concentration brings about an even greater calming of the prana, or breath, allowing yet deeper focusing of the mind, and so on. The final stage of this cycle is the complete withdrawal of life-current from the body and senses, and total concentration of the mind.

In very deep meditation the prana can become completely focused at the spiritual eye, and the body's need for oxygen and breath ceases. At first this may be a somewhat odd and even frightening experience, but it is the doorway to the deepest states of meditation. In fact, Paramhansa Yogananda defined a "master" as one who is able to stop his breath at will. Don't worry about this happening prematurely. It is a very deep state and not at all easy to achieve. If you do so, you will be ready for it. Most people, however, get great benefit from their breath becoming calm even if it doesn't stop altogether. Since the breath, the prana, and the mind are linked, this technique leads to a state of deep concentration.

You can think of this technique as a kind of bridge allowing a shift from the more physical aspects of our being, represented by the breath, to a calm and inward consciousness. Practice it for at least five minutes or even longer if you are enjoying the deep state of peace and joy that it brings.

8   End your practice of this technique by taking a deep breath and exhaling three times. Then concentrate very deeply in the area of the spiritual eye, leaving behind any thought of the body, and holding your mind completely still. With the mind deeply concentrated and interiorized you can now go on to the next phase of meditation where you focus on inner realities.

Normally the technique of watching the breath should take up about a quarter of your meditation. However, you may want to practice it for a longer period at first or when you are feeling especially inspired. Yogananda, as a young boy, would practice this technique for eight hours at a stretch! He suggested that those who want to become a master in this life practice it for two hours every day. How long should you practice it in any given meditation? Be guided by your own feeling of enjoyment and your ability to maintain your concentration. But remember, it is an extremely important technique designed to accomplish an absolutely essential purpose: total concentration. Without concentration, which helps interiorize the life-force, any time spent supposedly meditating is largely ineffective.

9   Watching the breath is different from many other meditation techniques, because it can be practiced at any time, even if you are not sitting still. Any time you want to control your mind, first control your breath! This is a great help whenever you are nervous. Try practicing *hong-sau* the next time you're in the dentist's office or before you have an unpleasant task to do. Once, as an experiment, I did a few rounds during a very tense scene in a movie. Within seconds all the anxiety had vanished!

Key Points
Watching the Breath

→ Sit with the intention of concentrating, letting go of all thoughts of past or future, focusing in the here and now.

→ Concentration should be relaxed, not tense.

→ Watch the breath, using hong-sau, or another word formula for about ¼ of your meditation.

→ Make no attempt to control the breath. Simply be an observer.

→ Whenever the mind wanders, simply bring it back to the breath.

→ When you end, keep the mind focused at the point between the eyebrows.

There are two more methods of achieving a state of deep concentration. The first, chanting, works with the verbalizing function of the mind while the other, visualization, engages yet another facet of consciousness.

Chanting

Paramhansa Yogananda often said, "Chanting is half the battle." A chant not only helps us to concentrate on a spiritually uplifting thought, but it also opens the heart. We will make little progress on the spiritual path until we can direct the natural love of the heart toward higher realities, and chanting is one of the very best ways to awaken spiritual fervor. Chanting also helps direct and focus the mind by giving us a clear focal point for our thoughts.

It is extremely difficult to go beyond the tendency to verbalize thoughts. Even when the mind is calm, this habit tries to reassert itself. Rather than simply repressing this normal mental function, we can use it to bring us into a deeper and more uplifted state of concentration.

A chant is a simple word formula set to music, often a prayer or affirmation such as, "From joy I came, for joy I live, in sacred joy I melt again." Most chants are devotional in nature and help to awaken energy in the heart center, and direct it toward a spiritual goal. Sometimes chants are sung in Sanskrit because of the inherent power in the sounds themselves, but for most it is easier to use

English or your own native language. By repeating a chant over and over, we focus the mind, open the heart, and re-program the subconscious.

Start your meditations with a chant or two. A very simple and beautiful chant sung often at Ananda is the one quoted above. You can hear this and other chants by going online at **www.crystalclarity.com/howtomeditate/resources.**

From Joy I Came

Words from Parmahansa Yogananda
music, unknown

Start by singing the chant out loud in order to awaken energy. After a few repetitions, sing the words more quietly and then silently, but with ever deepening concentration. Let the words be a devotional carrier beam connecting you and God. Ask Him, with all the intensity of heart and soul, to let you feel His joy. Gradually, let the words become secondary to the emotion (*bhav* in Sanskrit) you are wanting to express. Finally you can pass beyond words altogether, and speak to God with only the voice of your heart's yearning. It is in this charged atmosphere that He will come to you.

Chanting silently can also be done toward the end of your meditation, after you are deeply concentrated. Each chant emphasizes a slightly different coloration of the multi-hued relationship with the Infinite. A favorite chant of Yogananda's, *O God Beautiful*, is very good for increasing one's devotion. One night, after someone falsely claimed that Americans have no devotion, Paramhansa Yogananda led an overflow crowd at New York's Carnegie Hall for over two hours repeating this inspiring chant. The words are:

> O God beautiful, O God beautiful,
> At Thy feet, O I do bow!
> O God beautiful, O God beautiful,
> In the forest Thou art green,
> In the mountain Thou art high,

In the river Thou art restless,
In the ocean Thou art grave.
O God beautiful, O God beautiful,
To the serviceful Thou art service,
To the lover Thou art love,
To the sorrowful Thou art sympathy,
To the yogi Thou art bliss.
O God beautiful, O God beautiful,
At Thy feet, O I do bow!
O God beautiful, O God beautiful!

You can hear this sung by going to:
www.crystalclarity.com/howtomeditate/resources.

Chanting is also an excellent way to stay inspired throughout the day. By mentally singing as you go about work or stand in line at the supermarket, you can transform even the most mundane task into a spiritual experience. The Indian term for repetitive chanting or prayer is *japa*, and is one of the most widely practiced ways to keep the mind uplifted. While it is good to chant inwardly even while engaged in other tasks, it is better if it doesn't simply sink into a kind of automatic "background" noise in your mind.

At the very least, try to maintain a devotional mood while chanting inwardly.

Playing a chanting tape rather than more worldly music can change the whole vibration of your environment and is an excellent way to keep your mind calm and joyful. Because of its power to reach into the subconscious mind, music is a much more important factor in influencing our moods than we realize. Once a student of Swami Kriyananda's purchased a tape of him singing chants and played it often in her home. Her three-year old child observed how it changed her mood. One time when she was about to chastise him, he ran and got the tape. With quivering lips, he handed it to his mother, hoping it would magically protect him from whatever punishment she had in mind.

The environment we create around ourselves has a tremendous effect on us. In fact, Yogananda often used to say, "Environment is stronger than will power." By creating whenever possible a spiritualized or peaceful environment, we keep our minds uplifted so that the "programs" we receive from the Infinite are elevating. In the *Further Explorations* section at the end of the book, we have listed several CDs of chanting. We also operate a web-based radio program, **www.radioananda.org**, that plays chants, spiritually uplifting music, audiobooks and a wide variety of lectures.

❧ Every chant has an underlying mood or "*bhav*." Choose one that will express the quality you want: will power, joy, devotion, compassion, etc. Repeat the chant over and over for several minutes.

❧ Start by singing out loud, gradually getting softer but more inward and focused, and then continuing silently.

❧ Try to get beyond mere words into an expression of your own deepest yearnings.

❧ Silent chanting can also be done toward the end of meditation as a way to stay focused inwardly and prevent the mind from drifting around aimlessly.

❧ Group chanting, or *kirtan*, is wonderful. If there is no group near you, chant along with one of our CDs.

Visualization

This is another powerful method of focusing the mind for meditation. Visualization bypasses the verbalizing functions of the brain and therefore helps enormously to focus and calm the mind. In deep meditation visions occur spontaneously, and it is in this manner that God often appears to saints.

One way to experience an expansion of consciousness is to visualize a scene such as an expanding light, as in the exercise given next. This technique should be done later in meditation, after you have become relaxed and concentrated, having finished with watching the breath.

Visualize a blue light at the point between the eyebrows. If you can't see a light, then imagine one. When you perceive the light clearly, let it expand, first filling the whole of your brain, and then gradually infusing every cell of your body. See it continue to expand until it fills the room in which you are sitting, then your house, your whole neighborhood, your state, your country, and finally the entire earth. Watch the earth, as if from outer space, as it floats in your sea of blue light.

Feel that this light is uniting everyone on the planet, producing a glow of harmony and love. Now, continue to expand the light until it fills the whole solar system, then the whole universe. See stars and galaxies floating in the ocean of blue light like little points of white light. Feel that you, too, are resting in that sea of light and, in fact, *are* that light. Your body has expanded to become the universe and everything in it. The stars are your cells. Feel the great peace, security, and joy of this state. You need nothing because you *have* everything. Nothing can harm you because you *are* everything. Float in the joy of this universal consciousness for as long as you can, then gradually let the light condense until it again becomes a spot at the point between the eyebrows.

Swami Kriyananda has recorded several visualizations such as this that are available on a CD with beautiful background music. (See *Further Explorations* section).

One of the best things to visualize is simply the face, and especially the eyes, of Jesus, Yogananda, or another saint that might be dear to you. The eyes are the "windows of the soul." By looking into those of a master, one becomes attuned to his or her consciousness. Try to see them very clearly, first by looking at a picture, and then by visualizing them until they come alive inside your mind. Commune with them, sending and receiving love and attunement.

Techniques that concentrate and interiorize the mind will normally take up the greater part of a meditation. Don't stop practicing these techniques too soon. Only when you are deeply concentrated and in a state of expanded awareness is it good to drop techniques and simply immerse yourself in the experience. If any mental restlessness remains, the techniques you've learned will help you refocus and go deeper into a calm expanded state. On the other hand, concentration techniques should not consume all of your time, but should lead to the next stage, expansion. At least the final quarter of your meditation should be spent in silent inner communion with your own higher self and God.

Key Points
Visualization

- Choose an image that will deepen and expand your consciousness.

- Try to *feel* the scene as well as see it.

- Focus deeply until you become absorbed in what you are visualizing.

- Hold your image for as long as you can do so with concentration, and then return to focusing your energy at the point between the eyebrows.

The final stage of meditation is the expansion of consciousness. In fact, until this takes place, we are not truly meditating. In his little book, *Metaphysical Meditations*, Yogananda writes, "Meditation is not the same as concentration. Concentration consists in freeing the attention from objects of distraction and focusing it on one thing at a time. Meditation is that special form of concentration in which the attention has been liberated from restlessness and is focused on God. A man may *concentrate* on the thought of Divinity or of money; but he may not *meditate* on money or any other material thing. Meditation is focused only on thoughts of God and His holy prophets."

This distinction is vital. Concentration, a mental faculty, can simply increase the ego and therefore lead us further into delusion. True meditation, on the other hand, involves the superconscious and will always lead us toward truth. It is through opening ourselves to God that we draw the grace that changes us. Truly opening ourselves to God may be quite different from the type of prayers usually directed to Him. Mostly, these are requests—often, beggarly requests, for Him to fulfill some desire. God does, indeed, grant many of our prayers, especially if they are righteous requests. This kind of prayer is certainly a valid spiritual practice, but it cannot really be called meditation. The deepest prayers are for union with God—the goal of meditation. This requires first a stilling of our thoughts and desires, and then a release of egoic desires and self-definitions.

Inner communion is a merging of our individual consciousness with God or one of His qualities.

In practice, this means that after finishing with techniques that help focus the mind, we are ready for the final stage of meditation. Now, we should hold our attention on some aspect of the Infinite, such as light, love, joy, or peace. We might think of these traits as being qualities of a vast sea. Concentration techniques get us to the shore of the sea, but deep meditation requires that we enter the sea and eventually merge with it. We should spend as long as possible in an expansive state of consciousness, which can be experienced through either inner communion or devotion. Each involves keeping the already concentrated mind focused on an aspect of the Infinite.

STAGE THREE — EXPANSION

EXPANSION

Chapter 6

Devotion

Devotion is love that has been purified and offered to God or to a form of God, which Paramhansa Yogananda called "His holy prophets" in the quotation from *Metaphysical Meditations* above. Usually it involves the worship of the prophet or saint that is especially dear to you. Thus, a Christian would likely worship Jesus or possibly the Holy Mother, or one of the Christian saints. A Hindu might worship Brahma, Vishnu, or Shiva (symbols of God as creator, sustainer, or dissolver), or Rama, Krishna, or some other incarnation of the Godhead. Those who have found a guru might worship God as He manifests through that soul. God, the Infinite, can be worshiped through an infinite number of forms. Even though one religion or master may particularly appeal to you, it is good to remember that there is but one God who has manifested in every form. He is equally present in all religions and all souls. And he is present in each of us as much as He is in the greatest saint. The difference is only this: they have *realized* it! As our devotion deepens, we should try to merge with the object of our devotion. The best way to worship Christ is to become Christ-like.

Outward worship sometimes involves elaborate rituals or ceremonies. These may help awaken zeal, but unless the awakened energy is more inwardly directed, we will remain unchanged. Meditative devotion is much deeper. It tries to attune the worshiper with the *consciousness* of the form you love rather than merely its outward expression. Try to draw the consciousness of the master into your own. You can worship God in whatever form is dearest—mother, father, lover, friend—but don't hold Him at a distance. Converse lovingly with Him and share the innermost secrets of your heart. Give Him your joys, your defeats, your possessions and attachments. Finally, through your stilled mind and open heart, try to listen sensitively for a response to your devotion. God wants what is best for us, what will make us truly happy. In the quiet of meditation, toward the end, try to receive specific answers for your questions, or reassurance about whatever might be troubling you. Ultimately, it is your own highest self that you are reaching toward.

There is a story in India of a man who was worshiping his guru by offering rose petals before his picture. In the middle of his practice, the man suddenly started throwing the petals on his own head, saying, "I see now that I, untouched by ego consciousness, am that which I was worshiping. I bow to the Infinite Lord who has manifested as both my guru and me."

To worship God in the form of a guru, concentrate on the eyes. If you have a picture, look at the eyes and try to feel that he or she is silently speaking to you through them. Then visualize him or her inwardly, taking away every mental and emotional barrier. Draw that holy, loving influence into your heart and soul. Try also, during the day, to keep this loving connection active and vibrant.

- Choose whatever form of God is most appealing to you. Accept and appreciate that others may validly worship God in a form that is different from yours, but equally adored by them.

- Commune with Him or Her through the eyes. Hold nothing back. Give Him your problems, your defeats, and your victories.

- Don't hold God at a distance. Feel that He is the nearest of the near and the dearest of the dear.

- Accept His love for you and let it nourish and transform your life.

Inner Communion—Meditating on the Qualities of the Soul

Our soul might be defined as an individual spark of the Infinite. The true Self is the soul, which, being eternal, existed before we came into a body and will continue long after we have cast it off. The soul perceives through intuition, that is, simply, knowing. But during the time the soul is incarnated in a body, it takes on limitations. During a physical incarnation, the intuitive power functions primarily through the five senses. This process is so complete that we (the soul) begin to think of ourselves as the body, thus accepting its limitations. As we go through successive incarnations, we build up layers of self-definitions, which are like veils obscuring our true nature. This is the definition of ego: the soul identified with the body and personality. The whole purpose of meditation is to break this false identification with its limitations, and return to the realization that the true Self is the eternal soul, and not the mortal body.

In a sense, it is like a dream at night, when we take on the identity of one of the characters in our own dream. During the process of dreaming, when we have no outside point of reference, our dream character seems to be the summation of who we are. It is only when we wake up that we realize the character, and even the dream itself, was merely a play of the mind. Self-realized masters liken earthly life to a dream and urge us to undertake those steps that will awaken us once again to our true soul nature. Yogic practices are especially designed to help break the soul's false identification with the body. Deep meditation works to break the illusive bubble of this dream life.

The soul, which is an extension of God, has certain innate spiritual qualities. One of the best ways to expand our consciousness is to meditate on these primordial aspects of the Self. The Indian Scriptures teach that there are eight primary manifestations of God: Light, Sound, Power, Wisdom, Calmness, Peace, Love, and Joy. Because each of these soul qualities is an expression of infinity, our consciousness naturally expands if we concentrate on any of them. These eight eternal qualities are avenues that can bring us to the goal of meditation: the realization of ourselves as souls, beyond the limiting definitions of the ego. Meditating on the qualities of our true self is one of the most effective ways to achieve Self-realization.

After finishing the important but preliminary techniques of concentration, spend some time immersing yourself in whichever of these eight qualities most attracts you. If it is love, for instance, start by feeling a sense of love in your heart. *Feeling* love in the heart is more powerful than merely affirming it or thinking about it. There is a wisdom in feelings that is vastly underappreciated. Nerves connect the heart and brain, and positive feelings in the heart will produce a similar response in the mind. If we want to uplift the mind, controlling the feelings is more effective than trying to control the thoughts. Thoughts follow feelings!

To attune yourself to Infinite love, start by sensitively feeling that vibration of love in the heart. Don't personalize it, that is, don't confine it to any one individual or group. Simply try to get in tune with a universal expression of love. Work with what you actually feel, and then try to let it expand, feeling it first in the heart, and then letting the feeling also concentrate itself at the spiritual eye. This will connect these two centers. When you can feel it strongly at both places, let it grow until the aura of love is filling your whole brain, your thoughts, and then your whole body.

Now, realize that you are no longer able to contain this love in your own body, and let it expand out to touch those who are close to you. Don't let it stop there, for that would be too limiting. Divine love wants to embrace everyone and everything.

Let it expand to areas in the world where there is conflict or poverty, or anywhere in need of a special soothing balm of pure love. Let it also surround and infuse those individuals with whom you might have some tension. Don't allow any prejudice to block your radiating love. Feel that it is like the warmth from the sun that falls on everything and everyone, whether or not they are deserving. Finally, feel that this vast impersonal love is a living, vibrant, intelligent force that connects you to all living beings. Rest in this state of expanded love for as long as you can, letting it dissolve all sense of separation between you and "not you."

The final step is to realize that everything is made from the same one source of Divine Love, and that in reality, there is no "not you." You have become the sea of love itself. Even if you can't achieve this heightened state, the attempt itself will confer vast benefits. A little bit of this practice can transform your life.

As you go through the activities of your day, feel that you have an aura of love radiating out from the center of your heart that embraces everyone you meet. It might help if you feel that you are surrounded and protected by a bubble or force-field of love.

Each of the eight soul qualities is a potent, intelligent, living force. Saints of all ages and religions have experienced seeing a great light when in an ecstatic state. The Old and New Testaments of the Bible contain over a hundred references to light. The inner light of the spiritual eye will be seen in the forehead, at the point between the eyebrows, when the mind is calm and focused. This is the meaning of the passage in the Bible that says, "The light of the body is the eye: If therefore thine eye be single, thy whole body shall be full of light." (Matthew 6:22)

When the mind becomes very still you may see the spiritual eye itself, which appears as a white five-pointed star inside a blue field surrounded by a golden ring. If the mind is less calm, you may see a somewhat distorted form of the spiritual eye such as a donut-shaped ring, or see just an intensification of light and color in the forehead. Whatever you see, observe it calmly, increasing the intensity of your concentration until you become absorbed into the inner light.

It is very helpful to try to project your consciousness through the light into infinity beyond. In near-death experiences, one of the things most commonly reported is traveling through a tunnel into a great light. This is also experienced in very deep meditation, when the energy is withdrawn from body consciousness and expanded into Cosmic Consciousness.

Sound and light are much the same—energy manifested through various wavelengths of vibration. As in watching the inner light, you can listen to the inner sounds. Mystics of every religion have heard God expressed as sound. The various sounds associated with religion such as bells, harps, and flutes are, in fact, outward expressions of similar sounds produced by the chakras and heard in deep meditation. Listening to the inner sounds is very uplifting but, like seeing the inner light, requires considerable stillness of the mind. To hear the inner sounds more clearly, it is helpful to close the ears with the thumbs or use earplugs. Whatever inner sound you hear, try to listen with great intensity, first becoming absorbed in the sound, and then feeling it spreading throughout the body, dissolving all sense of ego and separation from God.

In attuning yourself with any aspect of God, be it light, sound, love, joy, or any of the other qualities, start with what you are *already experiencing* and expand on that. If you aren't able to see, hear, or feel anything, then remember or imagine an experience as a way of "priming the pump." For example, in order to expand into universal love, start with an experience of love you remember and let it grow, like a small ember glowing brighter until it bursts into flame and finally grows into an all-consuming blaze.

The little light seen in the forehead can expand to become the energy that manifests the whole of creation. The smallest trace of love or peace felt in the heart can be expanded until it embraces everyone you know. Then continue to expand that love to all people, all creatures, and finally everything in creation, animate or inanimate. By absorbing the consciousness in any of these eight qualities, one becomes attuned to God, who produces them.

True meditation is deep concentration or absorption in any of these qualities. And true spirituality, beyond any outward religious form, is unity with Spirit that comes from shifting your sense of I-ness from your little personality to Infinity itself.

The ultimate state of expansion is known as *samadhi* in Sanskrit. In this state you no longer perceive any sense of separation between yourself and the Infinite. That is, you are no longer identified with the limitations of the ego, or as a person who is isolated from others. You do not merely think, but *know,* that everything in creation is an expression of one Infinite Consciousness, of which you are a part. Yogananda's poem *Samadhi* is one of the clearest descriptions of this profound state that has ever been written, and is one of the most beautiful mystical poems ever penned. He suggested that disciples memorize it and repeat it daily to help prepare the mind for this experience.

We have included a free MP3 recording of Swami Kriyananda reading the entire poem on the special website:

www.crystalclarity.com/howtomeditate/resources

His poem begins with these lines:

> *Vanished the veils of light and shade,*
> *Lifted every vapor of sorrow,*
> *Sailed away all dawns of fleeting joy,*
> *Gone the dim sensory mirage.*
> *Love, hate, health, disease, life, death,*
> *Perished these false shadows on the screen of duality.*
> *Waves of laughter, scyllas of sarcasm, melancholic whirlpools,*
> *Melting in the vast sea of bliss.*
> *The storm of maya stilled*
> *By magic wand of intuition deep.*
> *The universe, forgotten dream, subconsciously lurks,*
> *Ready to invade my newly-wakened memory divine.*
> *I live without the cosmic shadow,*
> *But it is not, bereft of me;*
> *As the sea exists without the waves,*
> *But they breathe not without the sea.*
> *Dreams, wakings, states of deep* turiya *sleep,*
> *Present, past, future, no more for me,*
> *But ever-present, all-flowing I, I, everywhere.*

Key Points

Meditating on the Aspects of God

- Choose whichever is the most appealing of the eight qualities of God: Light, Sound, Power, Wisdom, Calmness, Peace, Love, and Joy. Remember, focus on only one at a time.

- Focus on the *feeling* of the quality itself, rather than merely thinking about it. Perceive it first in the heart and then at the spiritual eye, located between the eyebrows.

- Let the chosen quality expand until it embraces your whole body, and then in ever-widening circles, eventually, encompasses all of creation.

- Be absorbed in this expanded state for as long as possible, keeping your thoughts and emotions completely still.

- Hold on to the aura of this quality throughout your daily activities.

Intuitive Answers to Problems

Many people make the mistake of pondering their problems while trying to meditate. As long as the mind remains restless, one will neither be able to meditate properly, nor solve problems successfully. But once the mind has been focused and the consciousness expanded, intuition becomes more active and can be a great help in resolving life's dilemmas. Problems in life arise because of our limited understanding, and it is nearly impossible to solve a problem as long as our consciousness remains on the same level on which the problem was created. When we raise the level of our consciousness, the solution is often immediate and obvious. Wait until the end of your meditation when your level of consciousness is more elevated before trying to introduce questions.

Here is a method for finding intuitive solutions to problems: First, meditate deeply until your mind is very calm and centered. Next, ask for insight and solutions. Try to simplify and clarify your question—sometimes an answer becomes obvious simply because the question has been clarified. When you have a clear, simple question, project it through the spiritual eye as if you were broadcasting it to the universe. Ask your question with great intensity, and deep concentration, but without any mental agitation. That is, don't focus on difficulties but, rather, on solutions. Now, *expecting an answer*, concentrate at the heart center and be intently receptive. Often you will simply know the answer to your question. If no solution comes, pose the most logical alternatives and *feel* the energy in the heart. Does one solution produce a sense of nervousness or tension, and the other a feeling of peace? If so, accept the answer that brings peace. In order to feel clearly you must be very objective—holding on to an attachment or even a preference for one solution over another will inhibit the flow of intuition.

Ending Your Meditation

Always end your meditation with a prayer. You may want to pray for God's light to solve a difficulty, or to heal an illness if that is His will for you. Pray with the attitude that God *wants* to answer your prayer, and that you are His own child, His dearest friend, and not some insignificant beggar. You may want to end your meditation by simply praying for the grace to be able to feel the peace and joy of meditation throughout your daily activities. A very good practice that we personally do daily, is to pray for friends and loved ones. Finally, we always end our meditations by sending out love, peace, and harmony to everyone in the world, and praying that God's light touch every heart.

Key Points

Intuitive Answers

* First, meditate until your mind and emotions are very calm. Don't ruminate on questions or problems that will block your ability to go deep.

* Simplify and clarify the question.

* Project the question through the spiritual eye expecting an answer.

* Feel for an answer in the heart.

* If you don't get an intuitive answer, pose the logical alternatives. Feel for the one that has sense of rightness or calmness as opposed to a sensation of excitement or tension.

Transition to Activity
Chapter 7

Carry the peace and joy you feel in meditation into your daily life. Stay quiet and centered following meditation, extending the calmness into every aspect of life. When you realize that activity and meditation are really one, you will be able to find a still center at the heart of even the most trying circumstances.

The first few minutes after meditation are especially important. Keep silence, if possible, and go about your tasks calmly while holding onto the inward peace of meditation. Feel that you are merely playing a role on God's stage, owning nothing and no one, being only the caretaker of the possessions and people that have been placed in your hands. Often, after meditating, one finds colors to be brighter than normal, people to be more lovable, and events more "in-joyable." Hold on to this portable paradise for as long as possible, extending it into your commute, your work place, your whole life. This practice will give you a center of stillness during your daily duties and an amazing strength during times of trial.

In 1976 a forest fire destroyed virtually every home at Ananda Village. In the tense hours of the inferno and the confusing days that followed, the residents of the community were calm and even happy, never losing their center or their sense of humor. Our family lived in a geodesic dome that was aesthetically open and inviting. Unfortunately, its seams were also open and inviting. In short, it leaked like a sieve. After fighting the fire for several hours and seeing our home burn to the ground, I finally returned to where my wife, Devi, and our ten-day-old son were waiting. My words of greeting were, "Well, we don't have to worry about leaks anymore." Within minutes we were talking calmly about what happened and planning optimistically for the future.

For our family and other residents of Ananda Village, the daily practice of meditation had produced a state of non-attachment and inner joy that easily withstood what for most people would have been a major life test. In the days and months following the fire, we saw the fulfillment of God's promise in the Bhagavad Gita: "Even a little practice of this inward religion will free one from dire fears and colossal sufferings."

THE BASIC ROUTINE FOR MEDITATION — RELAX, CONCENTRATE, EXPAND

Chapter 8

Before you sit to meditate, you may want to stretch and relax by doing a few rounds of the deep yogic breath and/or the corpse pose. As you sit for meditation, check your posture. Be sure your spine is erect, your chest up and your shoulders slightly back. Relax the abdomen and be sure you are breathing from the diaphragm.

Offer a prayer to God, to those souls who particularly inspire you, and to your own higher self. Ask for the grace to be able to go into deep meditation and into inner communion with God.

Practice six to nine rounds of regular or alternate breathing to relax and focus the mind. Inhale counting to twelve, hold for a count of twelve, exhale to the same count of twelve. The rhythm can be shorter or longer according to your capacity, but be sure to keep the inhalation, retention and exhalation equal.

Then inhale with a double breath, tense the whole body until it vibrates, throw the breath out, and relax the body completely.

Repeat three to six times. Consciously relax the various parts of the body, starting at the feet and working your way up, part by part, to the head. End by relaxing the brain. Once you have relaxed completely, try not to allow physical restlessness to intrude again until you have finished the meditation. This process of relaxation as you sit to meditate, (not counting the preliminary deep yogic breath or corpse pose) should take only five minutes or so.

After relaxing, concentrate at the point between the eyebrows. Dismiss all thoughts from the mind and be completely centered in the here and now. Don't think about the past, or worry about the future.

Practice one or more of the techniques of concentration. You might start with *chanting*. First chant vigorously in order to awaken greater energy. Gradually become more and more inward until you go beyond the words into the silent yearning of the heart.

You may also want to do a visualization exercise. This can be done either silently within or by listening to a recorded visualization.

Now start the technique of watching the breath by inhaling deeply and then exhaling three times. Next, as you breathe in, mentally repeat "*hong*," and then as you exhale, repeat "*sau*." Practice this technique for approximately one fourth of your total meditation time, trying to bring your mind to a state of total concentration. When you find that your mind has wandered, gently bring it back to observing the breath. Try to deepen your concentration until you become completely absorbed and the breath becomes still. End the technique by inhaling deeply and exhaling three times.

Hold onto the state of deep concentration and calmness for as long as possible, trying always to go deeper into the inner silence. Gradually shift from the active "doing" state of practicing techniques to the receptive "being" state.

Inwardly attune yourself to the presence of God, one of His saints, or one of His eight qualities such as light, sound, love, joy, etc. Whether communing with God in a personal or impersonal form, try to dissolve all sense of individuality and separation. Become one with the object of your meditation! Hold this state for as long as you can.

Later, but while still in the state of deep calmness, you may want to ask for help or guidance concerning difficulties you are experiencing in your life. Broadcast your request from the spiritual eye and listen in the heart center for the answer. Expect an answer!

End your meditation with a prayer for yourself, for those close to you, and for the world. Pray, too, for the grace to feel His presence throughout all your activities.

Try always to keep your meditations fresh, energetic, and intuitive. Too little use of techniques will result in shallow meditations, but too much routine can make your meditations dry. Try to find the balance that brings you the most joy. Inner joy is the truest hallmark of deepening meditation.

SCIENCE STUDIES MEDITATION
Chapter 9

Scientists have been studying both the process and the results of meditation for more than a century. In recent years, however, the number of studies has increased dramatically. This is partly because both the medical and business communities have become acutely aware of the fact that stress costs billions of dollars each year. People are eager to find solutions to this pandemic problem, and studies are finding that meditation is the best tool available to counter stress-related problems. Researchers are finding that meditation, in addition to being a "stress buster," has numerous other benefits and is rapidly becoming a modern poster child for health. As a sign of its arrival into mainstream acceptance, meditation has been the subject of cover stories by many of the worlds' leading magazines.

Scientists and doctors are delving into several aspects of meditation. There are hundreds of studies on changes that occur in the brain during meditation, and others covering cardiovascular changes, immune system improvements, and a multitude of mental and emotional health benefits. Highly respected universities such as Harvard, Yale, and MIT; hospitals like the Mayo Clinic; and organizations such as the AMA are now doing studies on meditation and its benefits. Research involves many different types of meditation and covers both beginning and experienced meditators. The result of all of this research is a growing body of empirical evidence that verifies observations about meditation that have been noted anecdotally for years.

The scientific studies of meditation date back to the late 1800s, but by today's standards they tend to be relatively crude. Researchers could measure heart rates and oxygen intake but little more. Yet, even in these simple studies doctors were astounded to find yogis that could stop their breath for long periods of time with no ill affects. Some yogis were also able to demonstrate the ability not only to stop their pulse, but to have different pulse rates in the right and left wrists simultaneously.

EEG Brain Wave Studies

Beginning about 50 years ago, the development of more advanced instruments gave scientists a window into what happens in the brain during meditation. EEG (electroencephalograph) devices were used to record brain waves, and studies starting in the early '70s began to associate various types of brain waves with different states of meditation. Not surprisingly, they found that certain types of brain wave activity correlated very closely to the different stages of meditation—relaxation, concentration, and expansion.

Experimenters found that not only during meditation, but also after, there were shifts in the intensity and frequency of alpha, beta, theta, and gamma waves. Each type of wave is associated with certain kinds of activities as well as different neurotransmitters.

Alpha waves are associated with the closing of the eyes and a relaxation of the entire nervous system. When the brain is activated by stimuli, Alpha waves normally become blocked. In meditators, however, Alpha waves remain non-reactive to external stimuli, which indicates a quieting of the reactive pathways in the brain, thus there is no dampening of these brain waves. One can relate this to the ability to maintain a state of calmness, which is the first step in meditation.

Beta waves also increase in frequency during meditation. Lower-frequency Beta waves organize and coordinate many pathways in the brain, and their presence indicates that the processing of incoming sensory information is quieting down. Higher-frequency Beta waves are associated with heightened states of attention and are very prominent, for instance, in adepts practicing hatha yoga.

The changes in the Beta wave patterns of meditators show a quieting of the mind coupled with a heightened state of awareness. This Beta wave pattern may indicate that the meditator is experiencing the second stage of meditation, a withdrawal from outer stimuli and an increase in inner concentration.

Activity also increases in Theta waves, which are present during tranquil states of consciousness, indicating a deeper state of mental silence and pleasant experiences. An increase in Theta activity is normally thought to activate emotions, but in meditators it is associated with the ability to dispassionately view the patterns and drives in normally subconscious levels of the mind. States of consciousness that express Theta waves help meditators gain deep insights and overcome old negative tendencies known as *samskars* in Sanskrit.

During deep meditation, experienced meditators sometime enter into Delta wave patterns, which is normally associated with dreamless sleep, and is also seen in babies. This indicates the ability to withdraw from outward consciousness but remain alert while doing so.

Perhaps the most important of all are Gamma waves, which are associated with a heightening of consciousness in the frontal lobes. Gamma waves become more powerful and better synchronized during meditation. Some scientists have associated their presence with a superconscious state and a greater, but impartial, awareness of one's self. These findings have generated a great deal of interest because they give scientists the potential to quantify higher states of awareness.

With EEG monitoring, it has also been discovered that there is an increase in correlated activity between the two hemispheres of the brain, termed "brain synchronicity." This is linked to clear thinking and creativity, and may be an indication of the enhanced intuition that is commonly experienced by meditators.

While these brain studies are extremely interesting, we must be careful about mixing up cause and effect. The West has a bias toward material causation. Among some Western scientists there is the thought that changes in brain activity *cause* states of consciousness. Yogis take the opposite view: changes in consciousness come first and then express themselves in brain activity, just as the thought to move your hand precedes the movement itself. Studying the brain is a little like looking at the windows of a large house from across the street. We can see lights going on and off in certain windows and associate that with increased activity in those rooms. So far, so good.

It would be a mistake, however, to conclude that turning on a light in a room *caused* the activity rather than the other way around. It is consciousness itself that causes an increase or decrease in brain activity or changes in brain wave patterns. This is apparent because consciousness has been shown to exist beyond the confines of the brain. Great yogis experience vastly expanded states of consciousness and supernormal abilities, as illustrated through countless seemingly miraculous events in *Autobiography of a Yogi*. There are also many validated accounts (some in near-death experiences) of people being aware of events taking place far away from their physical presence. If it is the brain that produces consciousness, these examples could not happen, taking place, as they do, far beyond the scope of the physical brain.

MRI Brain Activity Studies

In the early 1990s, scientists started using various types of brain scans, especially fMRIs (functional Magnetic Resonance Imaging), to study cerebral blood flow and, by extension, metabolic activity in the brains of meditators. Although these tests are somewhat expensive and difficult to perform, they give researchers an even more precise picture of what happens during meditation. Doctors also get information that previously could only be obtained through autopsies.

They find that meditation has a profound effect on the way certain parts of the brain function. These studies show an enhanced control over the autonomic nervous system, and prove that even the physical size and structure of the brain changes. It is now clear that meditation makes some structures in the brain grow and others diminish—a stunning observation. As these studies pile up, scientists are beginning to see that the range of benefits that result from meditation are nothing short of astounding.

Until relatively recently, the accepted scientific model said that the brain and central nervous system change rapidly during childhood and adolescence, becoming more or less frozen in place somewhere around the age of 20, and then start to decline in old age as brain cells die off. Starting in the early 1980s, however, there was a scientific revolution in this understanding. Scientists found that the brain, no matter what age, responds vigorously to how it is used, just as a muscle responds to exercise. The adult brain was shown to be quite changeable, able to grow and change in both its structure and function relatively rapidly. This new model of brain plasticity corresponded with what yogis had been saying for millennia. When Paramhansa Yogananda said in the 1920s, "Looking into the light of the spiritual eye changes the actual brain cells," people assumed that he was speaking metaphorically. These recent experiments began to show that he meant exactly what he said.

The brain in both children and adults responds to the demands placed on it in several ways. Take, for example, learning a new skill such as playing the piano. The first thing that happens is an increase in the number of cells in the portion of the brain associated with music and dexterity. Secondly, the interconnections in those parts of the brain increase dramatically, and finally cells in regions nearby are recruited to help.

Let's look at some of the brain changes that are particularly associated with meditation. There are two areas of special interest: the frontal lobes and the limbic system, both of which influence your thinking, your behavior, and who you are. The frontal lobes are located in the area of the forehead above the eyebrows, with the most important portion being the pre-frontal lobes at the very front. This is the most evolutionarily advanced portion of the brain, found primarily in humans, although also in a limited way in more evolved animals such as dolphins. The frontal and pre-frontal lobes are why we humans have a bulging forehead, and lower animals, lacking such a structure, have a sloping one.

The other area of special interest to yogis is the limbic system, a primitive portion present in both humans and animals. It is shaped like a crescent moon and is located deep inside the center of the brain. The limbic system is associated with survival instincts including the "fight or flight" response. It is also connected to primitive emotions such as rage, fear, and aggression. Brain scans show that when people get frightened, upset, or angry, the cells in the limbic system start firing wildly. People with over-active limbic systems show phobias, anxieties, and poor anger management.

How does the brain respond to the practice of meditation? First of all, due to the meditator's practice of concentrating energy in the pre-frontal area, the number and functionality of the cells in these lobes increase. MRIs of meditators show greatly enhanced activity here. The effects are both temporary (during the process of meditation) and more permanent as the cellular structures respond to the demands of meditation. Researchers have found evidence that meditation increases thickness in the parts of the cerebral cortex that deal with attention, processing sensory input, decision-making, and memory.

Meanwhile, the primitive limbic system also responds to the practice of meditation. As attention is directed away from this area during meditation, MRIs show reduced activity, an effect that lingers for some time. Studies indicate that meditators show a decrease in anger, anxiety, depression, and insomnia, and a much improved mood control. These long-term changes are completely consistent with what would be expected as the brain responds over time to the practice of focusing at the point between the eyebrows during meditation and shifting energy from the limbic system to the pre-frontal area. Meditators also show a marked increase in areas of the brain associated with cardiovascular control, learning, memory, and (not surprisingly) the ability to concentrate. The whole subject of meditation and brain function is evolving so rapidly and is so vast that it is far beyond the scope of this book. Suffice it to say that meditation is the best brain tonic you can find, and also the least expensive.

Meditation and Physiological Changes

Science has taken an interest in other non-brain health aspects of meditation. The respiratory and circulatory systems in the body show marked improvements due to meditation. There is a reduction in many of the blood chemical and hormonal indicators used to measure stress. Not surprisingly, a meditative practice also reduces levels of *perceived* stress reported by respondents.

For the respiratory system, meditation decreases oxygen consumption, heart rate, and respiratory rate—changes that are the opposite of those that occur during the stress response.

There are also major improvements in the circulatory system. Meditation can reduce and control blood pressure at levels comparable to widely used prescription drugs, without the damaging side effects. It also lowers cholesterol levels; studies of heart disease patients show that those who learn to manage stress greatly reduced their risk of having another heart attack, compared to patients receiving only medication. A study published in the American Heart Association Journal showed that meditation may act to reduce atherosclerosis, thus reducing the risk of both strokes and heart attacks, and is a significant help for those undergoing angioplasty and similar procedures. Meditation combined with yoga postures, a low-fat vegetarian diet, and exercise is able to reverse arterial clogging. In another study, meditation was shown to reduce chronic pain by as much as 50%.

Meditation and Emotional/Mental States

Meditation has been shown to restore energy levels better than a nap or simple relaxation techniques such as listening to classical music, and also helps with insomnia. Studies show that inner-city residents suffering from chronic pain, anxiety, depression, and hypertension who were trained in meditation showed a 50%

reduction in overall psychiatric symptoms and a 44% reduction in medical symptoms. For those with severe depression, meditation has been shown to reduce their relapse rate by half.

Many studies have suggested that meditation has a significant effect on symptoms of aging, with one study indicating that those who had been meditating for five years or more were as much as 12 years younger than their chronological age as measured by a reduction in blood pressure, better near-point vision, and auditory discrimination.

One extremely significant result of meditation is that it helps people make positive lifestyle changes. It has shown to be very effective in helping people overcome addictions to drugs, alcohol, and smoking, producing larger reductions than either standard substance-abuse programs or prevention programs.

There are significant cultural as well as individual improvements. Meditation helps regulate emotions, enabling people to get along better. For this reason it is now commonly encouraged by a multitude of major corporations who see meditation as a vehicle to improve their bottom line.

The study of meditation and similar practices, while still in its infancy, is rapidly coming into the mainstream. Astonishingly, only a generation ago there was serious debate among physicians about whether or not diet had any marked effect on health. The situation today is similar concerning meditation. While there may still be a few holdouts who debate its value, the beneficial changes are so profound and widespread that nearly all scientists now accept that meditation is extremely beneficial. Even a little practice of meditation is helpful, as almost all of the benefits occur with a relatively modest practice of a technique such as we're suggesting in this book.

A friend of ours, Dr. Peter Van Houten, runs a bustling mid-sized clinic in the foothills of the Sierra Nevada Mountains of Northern California. He has been a family physician for over 30 years and has seen thousands of patients during that time. Dr. Van Houten has about 5,000 patients, virtually all residing in a relatively small area in the California gold country. What makes his practice unique, however, is that about 5% of his patients comes from Ananda Village, which is dedicated to the practice of the teachings and techniques presented in this book. This gives him the special opportunity to see first-hand the health benefits of a lifelong practice of meditation and the healthy lifestyle that meditators tend to adopt, compared to the rest of his patients who live in the same geographical area and serve as a sort of "control group." Here are some of his observations:

1.   Typically, the veteran meditators appear and have the physiology of a person that is at least a decade younger than their chronological age—e.g., a 60-year-old appears to be 50.

2. Meditators appear to recover from injuries, surgeries, and infectious illness about a third faster than those of similar age.

3. Meditators rarely use recreational drugs.

4. I commonly see in meditators a lack of passivity. They make habit changes more easily than the average person, and typically ask for behavioral suggestions for treatment of any illness.

5. They have a lower than average incidence of mental health problems, and those that require medications on average use about half the standard doses. Treatment times required are at least 1/3 less than usual with medications for mental health issues. Many fewer end up on chronic therapy.

6. They are more willing to accept suggestions for healthy lifestyle habits.

7. Overall, they are much happier, which may be the most important of all.

APPLICATION TO DAILY LIFE

Application
Chapter 10

While meditation, by its nature, is a time spent apart from the concerns of daily living, there are numerous ways that the changes brought about by meditation can be applied to our outward lives. Among the most important areas that can be improved are relationships, work, and health.

Relationships

Little else in life brings us as much joy or as much pain as our relationships with others. We are constantly seeking fulfillment through friends, co-workers, and spouses or significant others. Yet most of the "choices" we make in our relationships are conditioned by individual past tendencies operating on a subconscious level, and by the magnetism of the cultural environment in which we live. Most of the time we *react* rather than act. Meditation centers us, strengthens our powers of discrimination, and reduces our vulnerability to the hidden persuaders of society. Through meditation we are able to become a *cause* rather than an effect. This is especially helpful for improving relationships.

Ideally, we should become aware of ourselves and others primarily as souls, rather than just bodies and personalities. This realization needs to be gained first through deep meditation, in which it is possible to experience our own deeper nature. It is then relatively easy to transfer that expanded awareness to others. When we begin to relate in this way, profound changes can happen in the way we see others and in how they respond to us. Instead of demanding, even subconsciously, that they fulfill our "needs," we can rest in the inner fulfillment and contentment that we experience in a meditative state. Thus cooperation replaces competition, and the joy of mutual giving replaces the tension of reciprocating demands. A great sense of relaxation comes as we realize that relationships are given to us primarily to help *us* learn and grow, especially in our ability to accept and to love. Relationships lived in this manner hold the promise of deep fulfillment. The marriage vows we take at Ananda end with:

> "*May our love grow ever deeper, purer, more expansive, until, in our perfected love, we find the perfect love of God.*"

There is a technique that can be done in meditation for attracting the right life partner. After you have achieved a state of deep calmness, concentrate at the spiritual eye and send out a soul call to God to send you an ideal partner. Don't concentrate at all on physical appearance, but only on the soul qualities. Now send out strong energy in the form of magnetism to attract a companion with qualities ideally suited to you and your journey. As your concentration and energy level become more intense, the power of magnetism will increase. Eventually, if the magnetism is strong enough, this "soul call" will find a responsive chord in someone else, and you will be drawn together.

This technique can be used not only to draw a loved one, but also to draw opportunities in other areas of your life. Once, during the Depression, Paramhansa Yogananda gave a public talk about using this power to find work. He told his listeners (many of whom were out of work) that if he didn't have a job, he would concentrate at the spiritual eye and "churn the ether" until the universe gave him one.

In both these examples, the power of magnetism is paramount. Meditation helps us increase our magnetism in two ways: quantitative and qualitative. The power of an electromagnet depends on the strength of the flow of electricity through a wire. The same is true of the flow of energy in our minds. When we are no longer dissipating our energy by scattered thinking, the power of intention that flows through focused consciousness can become, literally, infinite. As the power of our thoughts increase, so does their power of magnetic attraction.

This works, unfortunately, in both positive and negative directions. We have all seen unfortunate examples of charismatic, but misguided, leaders and dictators, able to persuade others to their way of thinking.

Meditation also helps us expand and harmonize our sympathies and thereby channel our increased magnetism in more positive directions. One of the best things we can do with our life is to become a positive force in the world, to be filled with love, joy, and compassion, and eager to nurture others. Merely asking the question, "What would God want me to do in this situation?" can profoundly improve our lives and the lives of others.

If you meditate with a partner or loved one, you might try this visualization in order to increase the love and harmony between you. Toward the end of your meditation, start with the same visualization on expanding light that you learned earlier. As the light begins to expand beyond your body, see it surrounding and infusing your partner. Hold him or her in this light until it fills every cell, every emotion, and every thought. Let the light join your auras together. If there is any difficulty or tension between you, let the light dissolve it until there are no more shadows. This same technique can be done at a distance connecting you and others with a harmonizing energy.

If there is someone who is trying to harm you, it will only aid his agenda if you return negative energy. Instead, send a flow of light. If the negative energy coming to you is strong, you can help to block it by visualizing a cross of light deflecting the darkness, or a protective circle of light surrounding your body.

Work

Work would be a lot more pleasant if it were seen as an opportunity for self-expression and growth, as a kind of meditation in action. One branch of yoga, called *karma yoga*, is described as "action without any desire for the fruits of the action." How different this is from the typical modern job so often fraught with boredom, clock watching, office politics, and tension between workers and management.

Here is a revealing question: if you did not have to work for economic reasons, would you continue in your present job? Would you continue to work at all? If the answer is "no" to the first question, there is something wrong with your job. If it is "no" to both, then more probably your attitude toward work is the problem.

Work is better seen in terms of what we can give to it rather than what we get from it, in terms of personal growth rather than personal reward. Some years ago at Ananda we were rebuilding houses that had been burnt in the devastating forest fire I mentioned earlier. Everyone was pitching in, and consequently we had people on the carpentry crews who could be described, charitably, as less than qualified.

One day as we broke for lunch, the crew was discouraged because we were actually further behind than when we started the day. The head carpenter on the project gave us all encouragement and a chuckle by saying, "Well, let's remember, we're not building houses. We're building *character*."

In addition to improving our attitudes, the techniques we've learned for meditation can be carried over into the workplace. In fact, the three stages of meditation—relaxation, concentration, and expansion—can also be applied to the workplace. The same techniques that we use to relax before meditating can be applied, in a modified form, while at work. Good posture, deep breathing, and gentle stretching will help you stay physically relaxed. Pausing for a few moments to close your eyes and watch the breath will immediately get you centered and concentrated again. When circumstances permit, a short meditation at lunchtime can be enormously helpful. Staying centered will help you be expansive and creative in your work, making work a way to grow, rather than a boring necessity.

People make a mistake when they try to separate their experience at work from their spiritual aspirations. A much more integrated life can be ours if we try to infuse our day-to-day activities with the same consciousness we gain from meditation. The law of karma says that life reflects back to us the same attitudes and qualities that we express. Love others, and life will give you abundant love in return. To have friends, be a friend. The best way to find fulfillment from your work is not to worry about what you are getting, but rather what you are giving. And, the fastest path to self-fulfillment is to entirely forget about yourself and to see that you are part of a beautiful and vast web of life.

Radiant Health

Paramhansa Yogananda said that the root cause of illness is the conflict between the soul and the ego: the soul trying to draw us toward an awareness of our unity with God, and the ego trying to convince us that we are separate individuals. The subconscious tension created by this opposition produces blockages in the flow of life-force, and ultimately, disease. Good health results from a strong unobstructed flow of life-force to all areas of the body; while illness, moods, apathy—in fact, all negative states—are symptoms of a conflict or blockage of the life-force. One of the great benefits of meditation is a gradual freedom from these conflicts as we achieve an integration of our consciousness. We are then free to experience our natural state of vibrant health and energy.

This is not to say that there are no physical causes for disease, for certainly there are. Rather, we should recognize that physical symptoms usually have their root cause in consciousness or habit patterns. At Ananda we have developed a system called *Ananda Radiant Health Training*. This system recognizes that illnesses, especially chronic illnesses, are multi-layered.

Basically, there are four levels: physical, energetic, mental/emotional, and spiritual. The "Radiant Health Training" system gives specific practices and techniques to regain control on each of these levels.

On the physical level there are three areas that can, when properly controlled, bring the system back into a state of balance. These are: proper diet, proper exercise, and toxin-free living. By bringing these three into balance, we can greatly affect our health, longevity, and quality of life. There is an enormous amount of material available about physical health, being not only an important goal, but also a national obsession. Yet, the basic principles are both very simple and very powerful.

Eat a diet composed mainly of fresh vegetables, fruits and natural grains, with some legumes, nuts, and milk products. A vegetarian diet is best, but if meat is eaten it should be used sparingly and consist primarily of fish or fowl. Keep away from sugar and overly processed food, and avoid overeating. Fasting one day each week is one of the best and easiest ways to maintain a healthy body. But, don't become a fanatic—balance your diet and then forget it.

A simple exercise routine will pay back many times its cost in time and effort. Try to exercise for at least 30 minutes per day. Any exercise that makes you breathe hard will be enormously helpful. Aerobic exercise unleashes a process of better circulation, cellular cleansing, weight control, and glandular rebalancing, which helps on both physical and mental levels. For most, the best basic exercise is simply walking. But anything you enjoy is the best choice for you. Yoga postures are not only a good physical exercise, but have the added benefits of giving improved flexibility and balancing your life-force. Some weight-bearing or isometric exercise is also important, especially for bone density. This is another good reason to learn and practice the Energization Exercises.*

Finally, on a physical level, avoid introducing toxins into your system. The three worst habits, and best to eliminate, are the use of cigarettes, alcohol, and drugs. Any of these will not only take years off your life, but will also greatly reduce the quality of life. There is so much information available about this subject that virtually everyone knows that these three habits are self-destructive. It is not easy to overcome them, but meditation can be a great aid in making healthy lifestyle changes.

On the second level of energy, we must recognize the importance of prana. Our health is good when our life-force is balanced and strong, but illness results if it is weak, out of balance, or blocked. Many Oriental disciplines such as Ayurveda and acupuncture work with these subtle currents. The flow of prana can be increased by certain techniques (several are given in this book) that help us consciously enhance and direct these currents in the body. Paramhansa Yogananda devised a set of exercises, called Energization Exercises, which help bring the flow of prana under

---

* *See chapter 11*

our conscious control, and send it to various parts of the body to re-vitalize them.

A second factor is our willingness on conscious or subconscious levels, which acts as a master switch. Energy is blocked when we say "no," but flows freely when we say "yes." To feel energetic, learn to say, "Yes!" to life. We will return to the question of life-force in the next section, but for now let's continue with the four layers that produce radiant health.

The third is the mental/emotional level. Our thoughts and emotions are controlled to a surprising extent by habitual patterns. Evolution has made the mind exquisitely proficient at perceiving, evaluating, and reacting to stimuli from the senses. This process of sensory perception, recognition, and reaction takes place constantly, as long as we are awake. But two people can perceive and react to the same input in surprisingly different ways—differences that are largely dependant on the attitudes and tendencies that we have developed.

Daily thoughts and behaviors are like radio programs that repeat over and over with slight variations, like music on your favorite station. Normally, our mental radio turns off only when we sleep at night. Most people have little control over what plays through their minds, but when we change underlying attitudes, like tuning into a new station—we can radically transform our mental and emotional programming. There are two very effective techniques for changing underlying patterns: affirmation and visualization.

Finally, the spiritual level influences our entire viewpoint. We have a sort of spiritual "specific gravity," determined not by religion but by our natural state of expansion or contraction. One might define spiritual maturity as the ability to identify with ever-wider circles of consciousness. People come into this world with an inherent "specific gravity" that ranges from dark, selfish, and contractive to joyful, compassionate, and expansive. Earlier we noted the beneficial changes that take place in the brains and physiology of people who meditate. Changing our brainwave patterns through meditation is the best way to raise our specific gravity. Meditation is the supreme tool for producing a sense of radiant health on physical, energetic, and emotional levels.

Key Points
Radiant Health

- ❧ Health problems, especially chronic ones, begin in the consciousness.

- ❧ There are four levels: physical, energetic, mental/emotional, and spiritual. All must be given due respect.

- ❧ A strong mind will increase the flow of life-force, which in turn, will improve the overall level of health.

- ❧ Meditation is the supreme healer.

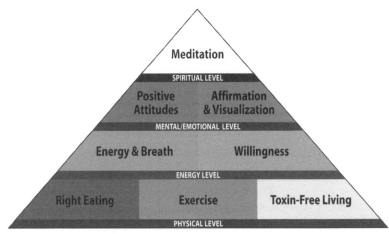

Radiant Health Pyramid

Directing the Life-Force

Many of the techniques given in this book help us to control and direct prana, so let's return to this subject. Life-force normally flows wherever it is needed without conscious control, or even awareness. Even when it is automatic and unconscious, will is the master switch that draws this prana into the body from its universal source, and directs its flow to wherever it is needed, to sustain the processes of life. But, through the use of will and yogic techniques, it is also possible to direct the flow of life-force *consciously* and energize the whole system, help heal an injured or diseased area, or heal others. The connection between will and life-force is especially helpful in dealing with repetitive health issues, because it gives us a way to help heal ourselves. The next time you are feeling unwell, you might try using this technique for healing:

Concentrate at the medulla oblongata (located in the brain at the base of the skull), touching the area for a moment with your hand in order to make it easier for you to focus on it. Visualize light entering at that point and then flowing down the spine. Now begin to gently tense and relax the whole body in order to flood it with light and life-force. Use your will to direct a flow of life-force from the medulla down the arms and into the hands while continuing to gently tense and relax.

Then stop tensing, and rub the bare skin of the left arm with the right hand. Do the same on the other side. Relax a moment, but continue to visualize the flow of prana into the hands. Now rub the hands gently but briskly together. The hands are very magnetic and have a polarity, the left hand being a south pole and the right hand a north pole. Rubbing them together crosses the poles and, as in a generator, produces a flow of energy. Raise your arms, hands upward, and feel the tingling sensation of the life-force flowing from them.

Place your hands on or near the area you want to heal, and using them as power sources, send healing life-force into the afflicted cells in a continuous stream. As you do this, try to visualize a flow of light into the cells. Continue until you feel you have filled the area with energy. Do this technique several times per day until the healing is finished. I know of many seemingly miraculous stories that attest to the effectiveness of this procedure.

A member of Ananda was once taking a day hike on a glacier in Canada. After several hours of walking, he slipped in a crevasse and severely sprained his ankle. It was so badly swollen that it was painful to put any weight on it and impossible to try to walk. Faced with the prospect of freezing to death after night fell, he placed his hands on his ankle and, for the next half hour with deep concentration, sent energy to the injured limb using the technique described above. After that time he was able to walk with only a little pain. A day or two later his ankle was nearly healed.

Several years ago another member of Ananda, a doctor, was in a very bad car accident in an isolated area of Mexico. Even though she had a crushed pelvis and many broken bones in her legs, it was almost 24 hours before she was able to reach a hospital. The doctor who operated on her said there was no chance that she would ever be able to walk again. During her recuperation, she used these life-force techniques every day, sometimes for several hours at a time, to send energy to her injured legs. Everyone in the hospital was amazed at her rate of recovery. She went home after three months, and today walks with only a very slight limp.

This same energy can be used to heal others as well as yourself. After you have energized the hands and can feel the flow of prana in them, place them on the body part of the person to whom you want to send energy. Concentrate on the *flow* of energy, feeling it as warmth, or visualizing it as light. Pray that God's healing power pass through you and into the person needing the energy.

Distance is no barrier to this energy, so this technique can also be used to heal people at a distance. In such cases, strongly visualize the person to whom you are sending the energy. After magnetizing your hands, move them up and down in space, sending waves of energy, and willing the current to pass into the recipient's diseased part. Continue this procedure for fifteen minutes, or until you feel you have accomplished your purpose. In a public situation where it would be awkward to use the hands, you can simply feel energy flowing from your spiritual eye into the spiritual eye of the other person.

For more information on the Ananda Healing Prayer Ministry go to:

www.crystalclarity.com/howtomeditate/resources

THE ENERGIZATION EXERCISES
Chapter 11

Paramhansa Yogananda devised a wonderful system called the *Energization Exercises*, which takes advantage of the power of will to draw life-force into the body.

The Energization Exercises are a system that can help you increase the flow of life-force and direct it to various areas of the body in order to strengthen and vitalize them. These exercises also help focus the mind, and are an indispensable aid to meditation. The whole system of 39 exercises is beyond the scope of this book, but, for those who are interested, we've put a link to an instructional video that can help you. These exercises are an extremely helpful aid, not only for meditation, but also for general health and vitality.

To see a demonstration of them on the web:
www.crystalclarity.com/howtomeditate/resources

It takes some time to learn the entire set of exercises, but many of the benefits can be gained from regular practice of only two of these, Double Breathing and Twenty-Part Body Recharging. Descriptions of how to do these follow. First, there are a few underlying principles that you will need to know.

1. Focus your attention at the medulla oblongata at the base of the skull, and feel that you are drawing energy from the universe into your body through that area. Just as food enters our body through our mouth, prana enters through an energy center, or chakra, whose physical counterpart is the medulla. Concentrate primarily on the *flow* of energy. Using concentration, direct energy to flow into various parts of the body by alternately tensing and relaxing that body part. For instance, to send energy to the cells of the left calf you would tense the muscles in that area. After tensing an area, relax and feel the result. This not only recharges the body with energy but, even more importantly, trains us to bring the flow of prana under our conscious control. Concentrate very deeply during the practice of these exercises. You can even close your eyes to help deepen and interiorize your awareness.

2. The tensing and relaxing of the muscles should be done in phases so as not to "strip" them. Tense: low — slight tension; medium — significant tension; high – strong enough to cause the body part to vibrate. Hold high tension for three or four seconds. Tense in a continuous wave: low, medium, high, and relax back in a wave: high, medium, low, completely relaxed. Concentrate on the center of the muscle or muscle group to which you are sending the energy, and always practice slowly, smoothly, and with deep concentration.

3. There is a spiritual law: "The greater the will, the greater the flow of energy." Feel that through the agency of your focused will you are consciously drawing and directing a limitless stream of energy. It is better to think of will as "willingness" in order to avoid making it seem grim. For maximum benefit, you should use your will very intensely, especially while tensing any area. Try also to be sensitively aware of the area as you relax and feel the result.

4. If a body part is ill or injured, use low tension only and send energy to that part, counting slowly to ten.

Repeat this several times. For internal organs, or body parts that you can't feel, you can send the energy mentally while visualizing the area. It is helpful to imagine a current of light flowing to the affected part.

5. Begin with a prayer: "O Infinite Spirit, manifest your spirit in my body as strength and energy, in my mind as concentration and determination, and in my soul as ever-increasing, every-new joy."

Watch a video of this exercise and others on the web:
www.crystalclarity.com/howtomeditate/resources

Double Breathing

With your arms out to your sides at shoulder level, exhale through the mouth and nose with the double breath that you've already learned, and bring your arms to the front until your palms touch. With a double inhalation through the nose, bring your arms back out to the side—tensing the entire body upwards in a wave from the feet to the head. Relax downward in a wave with a double exhalation, releasing all tension and bringing your arms back to the front. **Repeat this four or five times.** To review, double breathing is done by inhaling through the nose with a short-then-long inhalation and exhaling through both the nose and mouth in the same way.

Double Breathing

Twenty-Part Body Recharging

The twenty-part body recharging exercise has three phases. In the first phase, you tense and relax the whole body. The second phase consists of tensing and relaxing each of twenty different body parts starting with the feet and ending with the throat.

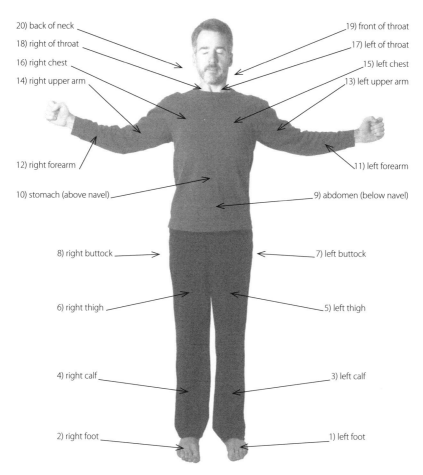

Twenty-Part Body Recharging

The third phase is like the second, except that instead of releasing the tension at each body part, you hold the tension in the muscles as you move up through the body. Then you release each part moving down through the body in reverse order.

Here are more complete instructions:

a) **First Phase – Whole Body Tensing.** Inhale with a double inhalation. As you do so, tense your whole body hard enough so that it vibrates. Hold the tension for three to five seconds, then exhale with a double exhalation and relax. Take a moment to feel the increased energy in the muscles.

b) **Second Phase – Individual Tensing.** Individually tense and then relax the twenty body parts in order:

19) front of throat	20) back of neck
17) left of throat	18) right of throat
15) left chest	16) right chest
13) left upper arm	14) right upper arm
11) left forearm	12) right forearm
9) abdomen (below navel)	10) stomach (above navel)
7) left buttock	8) right buttock
5) left thigh	6) right thigh
3) left calf	4) right calf
1) left foot	2) right foot

Just breathe normally in this phase. Again, as after the first phase, take a moment to feel the increased vitality that has resulted from the exercise after you have finished with the back of the neck.

c) **Third Phase – Accumulating the Tension.** Quickly tense (only to medium tension) the same twenty body parts, holding the tension in each part as you move up the body, inhale slowly as you do so, and when you have finished all twenty, inhale completely, hold the breath, and tense the whole body hard enough to vibrate. Now exhale completely as you relax the neck, dropping the chin to the chest. Then relax the remaining body parts moving down through the body in reverse order. Finish by feeling the sense of strength and vitality in the cells and muscles. Stand for a minute or so to relax and center yourself.

These may sound a bit complicated, but they will seem quite natural after a few repetitions. If you would like to see the complete set of Energization Exercises, including the twenty-part body recharging, contact Crystal Clarity Publishes for a DVD.

These Energization Exercises can be done as an excellent preparation before meditation, since they both relax and vitalize the whole system. The more you can get the mechanics out of the way, the more you can focus on sending a flow of life-force from the medulla area to the various parts. This ability to bring prana under conscious control is central to deeper meditation. The exercise can also be done after meditation or, indeed, any time that you feel the need for an energy boost.

Key Points

Energization Exercises

→ Energy enters at the area of the medulla oblongata near the base of the skull. Feel that you are directing a stream of life-force from there to the appropriate body part.

→ Tense the muscles smoothly from low to medium to high tension. Relax in reverse order. Pause momentarily between exercises to feel the increased vitality in the cells.

→ As you progress, concentrate less on the physical tensing and relaxing and more on the flow of energy to the part.

→ If an area is in need of healing, the life-force can be sent using the same principles but with low tension, or mentally only.

The Flow of Prana

The body is sustained primarily by prana and only secondarily by food, water, and air. It is even possible to live by life-force alone and dispense with food altogether. Paramhansa Yogananda, in his spiritual classic, *Autobiography of a Yogi*, gives examples of two people who existed on subtle energy alone and no longer needed to eat food. He wrote at length of his visit to the great Catholic visionary Therese Neumann, who lived her entire adult life taking nothing but a single communion wafer each day. This sustaining of the body through prana is the mystical meaning of Christ's statement in Luke 4:4 when, after fasting for forty days, he answers the temptation of the devil to turn stones into bread by saying, "It is written, that man shall not live by bread alone, but by every word that proceedeth from the mouth of God." Christ was able to consciously draw that subtle energy, or word of God, and no longer needed to depend upon food alone. The Energization Exercises that we just learned are a method of feeding the cells with prana.

In the unenlightened man, prana is involuntarily directed downward from the medulla into the astral spine. An enlightened master, however, is able to send the life-force from the medulla directly to the spiritual eye. From that point, if he so chooses, he can command it to descend into the body to carry out the necessary physical functions. Because the energy is under the control of his or her superconscious, it doesn't create identification with the ego, or karma. When a master wants to withdraw his consciousness from this world, he simply wills the prana to be redirected to the spiritual eye.

Our language contains a hidden wisdom concerning the directional flow of energy. The upward flow of prana is associated with uplifted and expansive states of consciousness, while the downward flow produces negative, contractive states. Every inhalation is accompanied by an upward flow of prana in the astral spine, and every exhalation with a downward flow. Interestingly, the word "inspiration" means both upliftment of consciousness and inhalation. We say we are "uplifted," "high," or "on cloud nine" when our energy is flowing in an upward direction. On the other hand we can feel "low," "depressed," " down," or "in the dumps" when our prana is flowing more strongly in a downward, negative direction.

Our body language also unconsciously reflects this. When we are feeling inspired, we tend to emphasize the upward flow by sitting up straight and by inhaling deeply. But when depressed, we slump and emphasize the downward flow with a sigh. Saints in ecstasy are pictured with their eyes uplifted, natural to a state of superconsciousness. The nimbus, or halo, seen in paintings of saints is symbolic of their energy having been lifted up to the top of the head and expanded.

But lest we get caught in the mere complexity of it all, it would be well to remember that in meditation we are dealing with a simple process. By concentrating at the point between the eyebrows, we automatically create a magnetism that draws the energy upward. Concentrate your mind one-pointedly on God, and everything else will take care of itself. As Yogananda's guru, Swami Sri Yukteswar, once said to him, "God is simple. All else is complex."

THE CHAKRAS
Chapter 12

As we discussed, prana flows into the body through the medulla oblongata. Prana is not physical energy, but a form of subtle, or astral, energy. As this energy enters, it travels down the *astral spine* and is dispersed into the body from six centers, or *chakras,* located along the astral spine. This subtle spine can be visualized as a tube of light running centrally through the body from the base of the spine to the brain. The central nervous system is the physical expression of the astral spine and, interestingly, has major centers near the areas of each of the chakras, where groups of nerves branch out from the spinal cord.

There is a vast and somewhat complex yogic science dealing with the chakras. Each chakra is associated with a quality of consciousness; an element; a planet; two astrological signs (one as the energy ascends and one as it descends); a sound; a spiritual quality; and so forth. As energy passes through or rests in any chakra, the mind is influenced by the qualities of that center. In the deepest states of meditation, all prana is withdrawn from the body into the chakras and then directed to the spiritual eye, enabling enlightenment to take place.

The following is a summation of the spinal centers and their qualities. For those who would like to delve more deeply into this fascinating science, there are several good sources available. Kriyananda devotes two lessons to them in his course, *The Art and Science of Raja Yoga.* A beginner's level book, *Chakras for Starters,* and a video, *Yoga to Awaken the Chakras,* are also published by Crystal Clarity Publishers. (See the *Further Explorations* section.)

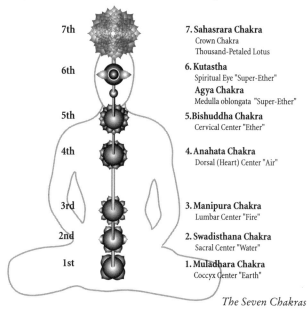

7th

6th

5th

4th

3rd

2nd

1st

7. Sahasrara Chakra
Crown Chakra
Thousand-Petaled Lotus

6. Kutastha
Spiritual Eye "Super-Ether"
Agya Chakra
Medulla oblongata "Super-Ether"

5. Bishuddha Chakra
Cervical Center "Ether"

4. Anahata Chakra
Dorsal (Heart) Center "Air"

3. Manipura Chakra
Lumbar Center "Fire"

2. Swadisthana Chakra
Sacral Center "Water"

1. Muladhara Chakra
Coccyx Center "Earth"

The Seven Chakras

1. Muladhara chakra

Location	Coccyx center, at the base of the spine
Element	Earth
Quality of Consciousness	Security
Spiritual quality	Power to avoid negative behavior or follow rules of yama (see page 148)
Inner Sound	Bumblebee
Planet	Saturn
Astrological Signs	Aquarius and Capricorn

A positive flow of energy at this chakra will result in firmness of purpose and the ability to avoid wrong habits and tendencies. A downward or negative flow will result in rigidity and anxiety resulting from an over-attachment to material security.

2. Swadisthana chakra

Location	Sacral center, in the spine opposite the reproductive organs
Element	Water
Quality of Consciousness	Sexuality
Spiritual quality	Power to follow positive rules or niyama (see page 148)
Inner Sound	Flute
Planet	Jupiter
Astrological Signs	Pisces and Sagittarius

An upward flow of energy here will help produce creativity and the power to do those things that are good for you. A negative downward flow will produce self-involvement and excessive sexual desire.

3. MANIPURA CHAKRA

Location	Lumbar center, opposite the navel
Element	Fire
Quality of Consciousness	Power
Spiritual quality	Fiery self-control
Inner Sound	Harp
Planet	Mars
Astrological Signs	Scorpio and Aries

A positive flow produces firmness of purpose and strong self-discipline; while a negative flow can produce the desire to control the actions of others and power struggles.

4. ANAHATA CHAKRA

Location	Dorsal Center, opposite the heart
Element	Air
Quality of Consciousness	Love
Spiritual quality	Divine love
Inner Sound	Bells
Planet	Venus
Astrological Signs	Libra and Taurus

An upward flow of energy in the heart chakra produces the expansive aspects of love: kindness, compassion, empathy, and devotion. A contractive, downward flow can produce excessive emotion and neediness.

5. BISHUDDHA CHAKRA

Location	Cervical center, opposite the throat
Element	Ether
Quality of Consciousness	Calmness
Spiritual quality	Calmness
Inner Sound	Wind
Planet	Mercury
Astrological Signs	Gemini and Virgo

An upward flow of energy in the throat chakra produces the calmness and the ability to stay centered in the midst of life's challenges. A contractive, downward flow can produce indifference to the needs of others.

6A. AGYA CHAKRA

Location	Medulla oblongata
Element	Super-ether
Quality of Consciousness	Ego
Spiritual quality	Divine Surrender
Inner Sound	AUM
Planet	Moon
Astrological Sign	Cancer

Properly balanced, energy gathered here can produce a galaxy of good traits—the expression of a fully integrated personality. An upward flow of energy toward the spiritual eye, the positive pole reflecting the medulla, produces a sense of divine surrender leading to Self-realization or union with the divine Self. Too much concentration of energy here can produce egoic pride, self-righteousness, and class-consciousness.

6B.   Kutastha—*Positive pole, reflecting the medulla*

Location	Christ center, at the point between the eyebrows
Element	Super-ether
Quality of Consciousness	Joy
Spiritual quality	Joy, Divine Will, Soul Consciousness
Inner Sound	AUM
Planet	Sun
Astrological Sign	Leo

Energy gathered here can produce enlightenment and joy. There are no negative aspects, which is one reason we focus here for meditation.

7.   Sahasrara chakra—*Thousand Petaled Lotus*

Location	The top of the head

It is the center of divine union. This center opens up only after the energy has been completely raised to the Christ center at the point between the eyebrows. Energy gathered at the *Sahasrara* produces cosmic consciousness, the realization that you are one with the Divine Source of all there is.

Summary of the Qualities of the Chakras

Meditating on the chakras has been practiced for millennia. Each chakra has a special gift to give us, and by attuning ourselves to the energy emanating from that particular area we find great inspiration and power. Yet, this practice is little understood by the general public.

Uninformed people mock the practice of "contemplating your navel" from a complete misunderstanding of an important technique. In fact, the concentration is not on the navel, but on the chakra located behind the navel. This chakra, being the center for personal power and self-control, is located centrally in the body, making it important in other ways. Some forms of martial arts have practitioners concentrate here and extend the inner power into their movements. Meditating on any chakra not only increases the magnetism of that chakra, but also helps to draw the energy up from the chakras located below.

In order to become more aware of the astral spine and the chakras, try the following: Place your left hand at the base of the spine and your right hand at the medulla oblongata (in the "hollow" at the base of the skull.) Visualize a tube of light, like a fluorescent tube, connecting these two points. If you sway your body gently from side to side while resisting the movement slightly it will help you to feel this tube more clearly. Now take your left hand and place it at the point between the eyebrows, visualizing the tube bending at the medulla and flowing through the brain to the frontal lobe. This "tube" is the astral spine. Each chakra is an enlargement of this central channel, directing the energy outward to energize the senses, muscles, organs, and systems that are fed by that energy. This is a simplified explanation of a deep and complex science.

For deep meditation, we need to withdraw the energy instead of projecting it outward, "Reversing the searchlights of the senses," as Paramhansa Yogananda put it. Any method of concentrating in the astral spine or meditating on any of the chakras will have a powerful, interiorizing result.

One of the most effective techniques for working with the spinal centers is the chanting of AUM at the chakras. AUM is the sound produced by the vibration of prana and is fundamental to the process of creation. One could say that the whole physical universe is brought into manifestation by this vibration or sound. In the Bible, the Gospel According to Saint John starts by saying, "In the beginning was the Word, and the Word was with God, and the Word was God." This "Word," or vibration, is a part of the mystical teachings of every religion, and each has a term for this holy sound. In yoga practices and Buddhism it is called AUM. In Judaism and Christianity it is called "Amen," and is "Amin" for the Muslims. To meditate on this sound is one sure pathway to higher consciousness.

Here is a simple technique for tuning into this great source of power and enlightenment. Start at the coccyx center, at the base of the spine, and slowly work your way up, mentally chanting AUM at each chakra. As you do so, try to actually *feel* energy at that point. It will help if you feel that the sound of AUM and even your breath is emanating from that center. When you reach the point between the eyebrows, concentrate there for a time and then slowly work your way down, again mentally chantingv AUM at each chakra. Do this, going up and then down, several times. End the final round at the spiritual eye, and then continue to meditate at that point for as long as possible.

Another valuable technique is simply to listen to the inner sound after the mind has been calmed and interiorized. By listening very intently, we can attune ourselves to the creative force of the universe, known in Christian literature as the Holy Ghost, or "The Comforter." Meditation and the comforting sound of AUM can greatly ease the stresses of life. This is an inward explanation of the passage quoted earlier from the Bhagavad Gita, "Even a little practice of this inward religion will save one from dire fears and colossal sufferings."

Key Points

Chakras

➤ The chakras are centers of power and are natural focal points for meditation.

➤ The astral spine is located in front of the physical spine. The six chakras are located in the astral spine like globes of energy, at the coccyx area, the sacral area, the navel, the heart, the throat, and the brain, which has two poles—one near the medulla and the other at the spiritual eye near the pre-frontal lobes. A seventh chakra is located at the top of the head.

➤ Each chakra has a particular sound, color, and quality (see page 138-141).

➤ Meditation on any of the chakras enhances the power of that center in our consciousness. It also has a powerful effect in interiorizing the mind for deeper meditation.

PATANJALI'S EIGHTFOLD PATH
Chapter 13

The meditation techniques we have been learning are part of the larger science of *Raja* (royal) *Yoga*. It is a science that includes all other branches of yoga within it, just as a king unites all provinces within his kingdom.

Raja Yoga's first written expression was by the ancient master, Patanjali, who is the most revered of all ancient exponents of yoga. Writing a few centuries before Christ, Patanjali explained yoga so succinctly that every teacher, from scholar to saint, regards his *Yoga Sutras* as the "scripture" of yoga. The *Yoga Sutras* consist of a series of 196 pithy statements or aphorisms, many only a single sentence long. These cover not only the path of yoga, but also the nature of the mind and, indeed, the whole of the human condition.

Far more than mere philosophical speculation, the *Sutras* come from revealed knowledge and serve as a road map for those who would explore the realm of Self-realization. Patanjali was an enlightened master, writing from a state of realization as well as practical knowledge. Other great saints who have followed the path of meditation to its end have experienced these same metaphysical truths and confirmed Patanjali's statements.

Patanjali's definition of yoga is both simple and profound. He writes, "Yoga is the neutralization of the *vrittis* of *chitta* (or the waves of primordial feeling.)." Although some translators use "mind stuff" for *chitta*, a better translation is "primordial feeling" because the fluctuations of delusion are kept active through the polarities of likes and dislikes.

The implications of this sutra are vast. In order to achieve a state of union, we need no book learning, nor is it necessary to participate in rituals, join a church, or achieve any exalted position. As soon as we can neutralize the polarities (Yogananda interpreted this to mean our attachments, especially), we automatically awaken to our true state—that of unity with the Infinite. In our intrinsic nature we are an extension of God, not a sinner forever damned to be separate from Him. Patanjali goes on to say, in the next two sutras, "When the vortices of *chitta* are neutralized, the seer rests in his true nature. At all other times he is identified with the *vrittis* (or fluctuations of *maya* or delusion.)"

It is a later section of the *Yoga Sutras*, called *Ashtanga* (eight-limbed) *Yoga*, that is particularly pertinent to the subject of meditation. In this, Patanjali outlines the steps that lead to cosmic consciousness. A brief review of these eight steps, which we will discuss next, will serve as a roadmap to enlightenment.

It can be helpful to see these eight steps as concentric rings. The first two outer rings give us the ten "rules" of moral principles for how to behave. Proper behavior helps create a harmonious life, which is a necessary foundation for enlightenment.

But it is not enough only to control our outer behavior—we must also learn to have a harmonious consciousness. The next three concentric rings show us the progressive control of prana, and the resulting interiorization of energy that allows us to still the mind. The final three rings describe the ever-deepening stages of true meditation, leading finally to *Samadhi,* or union with the Infinite. The techniques and philosophy presented throughout this book are based on Patanjali's eight-fold path and the more-inclusive science of Raja Yoga.

Steps 1 and 2 – Yama and Niyama

Patanjali's first two steps or branches, *yama* and *niyama,* give us the moral guidelines and attitudes we should use to direct our lives. It does little good to gather the milk of peace in meditation if the bucket of life is so full of holes that the precious milk immediately drains out. Westerners might tend to think of these first two steps, the *yamas* and *niyamas,* as being similar to the Ten Commandments of the Bible. But rather than commandments, they are more accurately seen as the basic principles that allow us to be in harmony with universal laws. To practice the five *yamas* and five *niyamas* properly one must understand that they apply to both outward behavior and inner attitudes.

Yama—Control. These are the controls or "don'ts" of life, the tendencies in human nature that end up creating disharmony and pain if allowed expression. Therefore, we must learn to control or stop the flow of energy in these directions. The five *yamas* are: nonviolence, non-lying, non-stealing, non-sensuality and, non-greed. Let's discuss each in turn.

a) **Non-Violence (***Ahimsa***).** If we seek a life of harmony, we must begin by controlling any tendency to act in a violent manner. In all the *yamas* and *niyamas*, the goal is to achieve not only outer control, but more importantly, a completely natural inner state of compliance. Thus, if we are to practice non-violence properly, we must not only outwardly refrain from harming any living thing, but we must also accomplish the more difficult task of overcoming any tendency to *wish* harm. When these inner tendencies, often subconscious, are finally quelled, we achieve a wondrous harmony with all life, and freedom from fear. If left uncontrolled, the tendency toward violence separates us from other living things and contracts our consciousness, which is the opposite of what we need for liberation. Patanjali explains that when one perfects any of the five *yamas* or *niyamas*, he develops a special power or *siddhi*. When we perfect the quality of non-violence, the whole world becomes peaceful around us.

There are numerous stories of wild animals becoming tame or responding peacefully in the presence of saints. Among the best known in the West are the stories about Saint Francis of Assisi. Using only the power of love, he tamed a ferocious wolf that had been harassing the residents of the town of Gubbio. A few years ago the skeleton of a large wolf was found buried under the floor of a church in Gubbio, lending credibility to the legend.

There is also the famous story of Saint Francis giving a sermon to a large flock of birds that gathered around him. Francis, perhaps more than any other saint, had a special attunement to animals and nature, as well as a deep practice of non-violence. Some of the most famous frescos in the world by the early Italian Renaissance painter Giotto, line the walls of Assisi's great Basilica of Saint Francis depicting in a series of glorious panels the most important events in the life of this beloved saint. One of the most charming is a scene of him blessing a flock of birds that has gathered around him. Francis and the birds look lovingly at each other while a brother monk looks on. Patanjali promises that the world around us will become peaceful when we, like St. Francis, are saturated with peace.

b) Non-Lying (*Satya*). One of the goals of the spiritual quest is to perceive the subtle truths of creation that lie beyond the scope of the rational mind. Without total honesty we can't hope to find infinite truth. As a starting point, we must first learn to control any tendency to *say* anything that is not truthful. This means even little white lies and exaggerations of the truth that nudge us out of alignment with what is. Once we have controlled our outward behavior we can progress to the deeper practice of complete inward honesty. This includes not only being truthful in relating to others, but also total self-honesty. We cannot grow by shrinking from the truth. The directive to be truthful, however, doesn't convey upon us a right to hurt others by blunt statements. Apparent facts often hide deeper truths, and we should be careful to discriminate before we speak. To tell a bed-ridden patient, for example, that he looks terrible, may be a fact, but it may also slow his healing process. Furthermore, in his soul he is well even if his body may be suffering. How much better it would be to affirm health to him while still avoiding saying anything untruthful.

The power that comes with the perfection of *Satya* is that whatever one says will come true. It was this power that allowed Jesus to call forth Lazareth from the tomb when all others said he was dead.

c) Non-Stealing (*Astaya*). We must work to curb the tendency to take anything that does not belong to us. This includes not only material objects, but also more subtle things such as praise or position. On the level of relationships, it means not to take energy, or even love, from someone unless it has been freely offered. The power that comes with perfection of non-stealing is that any wealth comes automatically when it is needed.

d) Non-Sensuality (*Brahmacharya*). Tremendous energy is expended through thinking about and seeking sensual pleasures.

Much of life and certainly most of what we call entertainment is designed to stimulate the senses. While *brahmacharya* refers specifically to sexual self-control, it also includes other sense pleasures. Yogic teachings don't dwell on sin or declare something wrong because an outside authority says so. Instead, yoga deals with the question of how to best direct our energy, and most especially, what will lead us to enlightenment. Here Patanjali is not saying that sexuality is sinful, but that the energy dissipated through excessive sensuality can be better used if it is freed and directed toward the expansion of consciousness.

Our true self, the eternal soul, perceives by intuition, inner knowing, which is inherently expansive. But while incarnated in a body, the soul functions through the mind and the five senses. During this time it takes on the inherent limitations of that way of perceiving, much as someone playing a video game has to take on the limitations of his game character. The great challenge is how to get beyond the limitations of the senses and back to our soul's intuitive state. This requires a withdrawal from the world of the senses.

Meditation techniques help quiet the sensory overload, but here Patanjali advises that we should also live our daily lives with a certain degree of control over the senses, thus helping to break the hypnotic power of sense stimulation. All perception takes place in the mind, but the senses make it seem as if it is all happening outside ourselves. To break this delusion, he advises us to keep our energies somewhat withdrawn. Paramhansa Yogananda said, "Touch is the most difficult of all the senses. When there is pain in the body, it is very hard to believe that the body is nothing but a mass of vibrations of sight, sound, taste, smell, and touch. " One problem with sensory stimulation is that it draws us away from peace and calmness and impels us to find fulfillment outside ourselves — an impossible task. The fifth limb (which shall be discussed later) is called *pratyahara*, or shutting off the sense telephones.

Meditation is, in large part, a conscious redirection of the outward flowing life-force in an upward and expansive direction. What we are really dealing with here is energy and magnetism. The spiritual eye represents the positive pole of the battery, while the base of the spine represents the negative pole. Meditating at the spiritual eye strengthens the magnetism at the positive pole, which leads to an upward flow of prana. Indulgence in sensory stimulation strengthens the negative pole and enhances the downward, or contractive, flow of energy.

Patanjali urges us, therefore, to hold the senses in check. The *siddhi* (power) that comes when we learn not to dissipate energy through the senses is tremendous mental and spiritual vitality.

e) Non-Greed (*Aparigraha*). Earlier we saw the reason for non-stealing, but now we learn that we should be non-attached even to that which we could rightly claim to be our own. Too many possessions create a kind of prison, first of material desire, then of attachment, and finally anxiety lest we lose what we have. It is good to discriminate between "needs" and "wants." Greed (wanting more than you need) stems from insecurity at some level of the consciousness. Part of growth toward spiritual maturity is developing a deeper faith in the power of the universe to sustain us. In deep meditation we see that we are now, always have been, and always shall be sustained through an outpouring of God's energy or grace. Possessions are simply divine Grace manifested in a physical form. To clutch greedily to a few possessions is like a man hoarding a bucket full of water while living on the banks of a vast river. Greed cuts us off from the flow of the infinite power. But lest this teaching make us passive, it is not ambition that we need to suppress, but rather the tendency to clutch the results of our efforts to ourselves. Spiritually, it is good to become successful, if we share with others the goods we have acquired.

An intriguing power comes with the perfection of non-greed. When you no longer have even a subconscious tendency toward greed, you can see your past, present, and future lives clearly.

Niyama—Non-Control. The five *niyamas* are the non-controls or the "dos" of the path, the types of behavior we should encourage in ourselves. The *niyamas* are cleanliness, contentment, austerity, self-study, and devotion to God.

a) Cleanliness (*Saucha*). Purity of body, mind, and environment is very important for harmonizing our energies. In all cultures, one of the signs of a more evolved person is cleanliness, and not just for such obvious reasons as controlling disease. The universe has a beautiful order and harmony to it, and among refined people there is an innate impulse also to create harmony and beauty.

Elsewhere, Patanjali lists "carelessness" as one of the impediments to yoga. The whole list of impediments is interesting, and is in itself a guide to proper action. They are: disease, dullness, doubt, carelessness, sloth, worldly-mindedness, false notion, missing the point, and instability. Why impediments? Because they block the flow of life-force and distract the mind.

There are also subtler reasons for cleanliness, things that can be *felt* if not seen. A great yogi from India, Swami Chidananda, once visited our Ananda community. During a tour of our gardens, he noticed a rusty watering can lying on the ground. "What is that for?" he asked. We explained that it was used for watering transplants. He paused for a moment and remarked, "Then you should pick it up, paint it, and have a place to keep it. Lower astral entities are attracted to clutter."

The *siddhi* that comes with the perfection of cleanliness is a disinclination toward things related to the body.

b) Contentment (*Santosha*). Contentment—being able to accept things as they are—is the supreme virtue. Happiness is determined much more by our level of contentment than by what we possess. If we constantly want more, no matter how much we have, we create a mental environment in which a host of negative qualities can grow—envy, jealousy, frustration, anger. The cure is so simple, yet difficult to actually practice: Appreciate life as it is.

I have long used an affirmation to help me overcome the tendency to grumble about life. It has proven amazingly effective, and you might want to try it:

> *I am grateful for my life exactly as it is.*
> *I am thankful for this day,*
> *I welcome every hour.*
> *Thank you, God. Thank you, God.*

Contentment does not imply that one should become apathetic or lazy. It means, rather, to accept that which we cannot change. The power that comes with the perfection of contentment is supreme happiness.

c) Austerity (*Tapasya*). We must learn to master our likes and dislikes, and to have the determination to do what we decide. Traditionally this *niyama* has been interpreted as the ability to perform austerities or difficult feats of will power. The Indian scriptures are full of stories about saints who gained magical powers through the performance of a difficult austerity. These stories seem, at first reading, to be talking about power over enemies or worldly affairs. When they are more deeply understood, however, they refer to power over our own weakness and ignorance. It is an excellent spiritual practice to take on a task that seems a little beyond your comfort zone, and then use unbreakable determination to complete it. In this way, your inner strength will increase until you grow strong enough to conquer the supreme foe: delusion itself.

Patanjali says various psychic powers come with the perfecting of this virtue.

d) Self-Study (*Swadhyaya*). Introspection allows us to see ourselves clearly with both our good and bad qualities. Self-study need not produce negative judgments, but rather helps us to be completely clear-minded and objective. Without introspection and self-analysis, it is impossible to progress very far on the spiritual path. Yet, it is not helpful to wallow in guilt and self-reproach. True self-study should help one to see clearly where he is and what he needs to change in order to grow.

The power that comes with perfection in this is the vision of that aspect of God that one worships.

e) Devotion (*Iswara Pranidhana*). Devotion is the turning of the natural love of the heart toward God rather than toward objects of the world. This love is the one quality that is absolutely essential if we are to progress on the spiritual path. If our devotion is strong enough, we will somehow manage, as many Christian saints have demonstrated, to achieve our goal even without techniques.

Perfect devotion brings the supreme state of *samadhi*, or divine bliss.

Patanjali says, "These *(yamas* and *niyamas)* must not be conditioned by class, place, time, or occasion." He means that we must not find rationalizations to avoid acting rightly. When we sincerely try to practice these ten qualities, there will inevitably arise occasions that will challenge us. Yet, if we persevere, it is the universe, not ourselves, that will have to readjust.

This profound and subtle teaching forms the basis of the law of miracles. It is our consciousness, working through subtle laws of magnetism that *creates* our circumstances just as it is God's consciousness that creates the universe as a whole. Consciousness, not form, is the ultimate reality. God's consciousness, acting through a pure channel (one firmly established in the *yamas* and *niyamas*), has the power to work any miracle imaginable.

The study and practice of these ten precepts is worthy of a lifetime of effort, and if accomplished or even tried sincerely, will certainly change your life. Imagine what a paradise this earth would be if people everywhere lived according to these principles!

Steps 3, 4, and 5 – Asana, Pranayama, Pratyahara

Asana. The next three steps lead to the interiorization of energy, which is necessary before we can really meditate. *Asana* (posture) is the next limb. Patanjali says simply, "The posture should be steady and comfortable. From this comes freedom from the assaults of the pairs of opposites."

One of the great sources of mental disturbance is the plethora of nerve signals coming from the body. That is why meditation starts with relaxation and proper posture in order to hold the body still. A restless body will inevitably create a restless mind. To accomplish perfect physical stillness, it helps greatly if the body is strong, flexible, and healthy. The science of hatha yoga (yoga postures) evolved from the simple need to keep the body completely still during the long periods of meditation needed to attain Cosmic Consciousness. When practiced correctly, hatha yoga is a marvelous science that produces amazing fitness not only for the muscles and joints, but also for the internal organs. The practice of hatha yoga also goes far beyond mere physical benefits, because as a true yogic path, it works to harmonize and uplift the life-force. In our *Ananda Yoga* system these more subtle benefits are emphasized. Each posture is given an affirmation designed to increase the flow of prana naturally produced by that particular pose.

Hatha yoga has become, unfortunately, too much of a merely physical science in recent years. Wonderful though it is for health and beauty, it should always be practiced with its higher purpose in mind: to lift us above mundane concerns and help us find God.

One time a hatha yoga adept came to give a demonstration of the postures to the great woman saint, Anandamayee Ma. As he was expertly going through a series of extremely difficult postures, Ma sat quietly staring off into space, hardly even bothering to recognize his presence. "Why," she was saying through her silence, "should

I pay any attention to this egotist who has perverted even this holy science into just another way of puffing up his pride." In the practice of the asanas, as in all things, let us reflect the words of Yogananda's beautiful poem:

> *In waking, eating, working, dreaming, sleeping,*
> *Serving, meditating, chanting, divinely loving,*
> *My soul will constantly hum, unheard by any:*
> *God! God! God!*

Pranayama (energy control) is the next limb. *Pranayama* is a combination of two words that should now be familiar: *prana* (subtle energy or life-force) and *yama* (control.) After we are able to still the disquieting sensations of the motor nerves through *asana*, we must then control the more subtle life-force through *pranayama*. Many meditation techniques, such as the *pranayama* breathing techniques we learned earlier, are designed to help control prana, since it serves as the bridge between the easily observed physical world and the more subtle aspects of the astral or energy body. When both forms of energy become stilled and internalized, we are finally able to concentrate deeply. Deep concentration at the spiritual eye energizes the positive polarity of that magnetic center. When that focus has sufficient strength and constancy it lifts us into the state of enlightenment.

Yoga postures are a physical means of directing the flow of life-force, especially when practiced as we do in Ananda Yoga. The

Energization Exercises are designed to accomplish this same goal. Both, being physical and therefore outward, are relatively easy to practice, but because they influence prana, they accomplish much more that it seems on the surface.

Pranayama is a vital stage because it forms a bridge between body and mind, allowing us to still the consciousness. There is a final cause of disturbance to the mind that Patanjali addresses next.

Pratyahara (sense control). In the *Yoga Sutras* Patanjali says, "*Pratyahara* is the withdrawing of the mind and senses from the objects of the senses. Then follows the greatest mastery over the senses." Paramhansa Yogananda called this final preparatory stage before deep meditation "shutting off the sense telephones."

The signals sent by the sensory nerves to the brain are one of the main causes of mental restlessness, and are a great obstacle to stilling the mind. It is very helpful to do whatever you can outwardly to shut off the senses. Closing the eyes shuts off most of the signals from the optic nerves. The next biggest source of disturbance is noise, and many meditators use earplugs or headphones to reduce sound. By holding the body completely still, we diminish the sense of touch. To dull the sense of smell, some also like to burn incense. Paradoxically, creating a steady state of stimulation is another way of helping the mind to disregard stimulation from the senses. Taste is naturally quiescent, or at rest, unless it is stimulated on purpose.

Yet one can only go so far to shut off *outward* causes of distraction. I remember once, under very silent conditions, being disturbed by the sound my eyelids made when I blinked! True *pratyahara* occurs in the mind, not the body. It is the internalization of the life-force (*pranayama*) that results in the shutting down of the sense telephones, a natural process that happens every night as we fall asleep.

With these three stages; *asana, pranayama,* and *pratyahara,* we have eliminated the sources of mental agitation and set the stage for deep meditation. The stages of increasingly deep meditation are: *dharana* (concentration), *dhyana* (absorption), and *samadhi* (bliss).

Steps 6, 7, and 8 – Dharana, Dhyana, Samadhi

Dharana (Concentration). This is the ability to bring the mind into focus and to hold the concentration on a single point. In a sense, everything that we have learned up to this point is a means of achieving and maintaining this state. In true *dharana* all body-consciousness and restless thoughts cease, enabling us to focus on the object of our meditation without distraction. If, for instance, we are meditating on a light at the spiritual eye, we will be completely focused on the light and have no competing thoughts to disturb us. The reason we practice the technique of *hong-sau,* or watching the breath, is to achieve the stillness necessary to arrive at the state of *dharana*. Lest we set the goal impossibly high, any deepening of concentration, even if it is only partial or fleeting, is extremely beneficial. Virtually all of the benefits we talked about in chapter nine, "Science Studies Meditation," are ours even though our concentration is imperfect. To simply hold the energy and concentration at the point between the eyebrows will change the brain and consciousness.

Yet, the final goal is one-pointed focus. There is a wonderful story from the great epic, *The Mahabharata*. Arjuna, who represents the ideal devotee, is the finest archer in the land. Archery here is a symbol for meditation, the arrows representing concentration. In the story, Dronacharya, the teacher of archery (meditation), is holding a contest. There is a statue of a vulture placed high in a tree, and its head is the target. As each student approaches to take his turn Dronacharya asks him what he sees. One replies, "I see you, my teacher, the tree, the sky, and all who have gathered around." This student misses his shot. The next replies in a similar manner, and he, too, misses.

Finally, after everyone else has failed to hit the target, Arjuna approaches. In response to the question he answers, "I see the head of the bird."

Dronacharya asks, "Don't you see anything else?"

Arjuna replies, "I see only the head of the bird."

He, of course, hits what he sees. This story illustrates the state of *dharana* or absolute concentration. When we can achieve the stage of *dharana* and hold it for some time we will automatically move to the next stage, *dhyana*.

Dhyana (Absorption). Here Patanjali is speaking about the ability to merge with the object on which you are concentrating. Let's return to the example we used, of meditating on the light of the spiritual eye, and see how a person would describe his meditation after he had finished. If one had achieved the state of *dharana*, or concentration, he would say something like, "I had an incredibly deep meditation. I saw a light at the spiritual eye and was able to focus on it completely. For a long time there were no other distracting thoughts in my mind. It was wonderful."

Holding onto this state for a period of time leads naturally to the stage of *dhyana* where we merge into the light so completely that we perceive ourselves *as* that light. Light would simply fill our consciousness and we would no longer think of ourselves as looking at something. After a meditation of this depth, our friend would report, "First, I was looking at the light. Then, as I held my attention on it, I seemed to become the light. It was as if I somehow merged into it."

Earlier, we learned the practice of meditating on one of the eight qualities of the soul, or our divine nature. Any of these gives us a focal point for concentration, helping us arrive at the state of *dharana*. When we become totally absorbed in any of these qualities, we reach the higher state of *dhyana*. This absorption will seem perfectly natural, when it happens, because we are merging back into our own soul nature. In another of the *Yoga Sutras*, Patanjali says that yoga (union) is "memory." We don't have to *learn* who we are, but simply *remember*. *Dharana* and *dhyana* eliminate the mental static that has prevented us from remembering our own true self. When we see that we need not be limited to the confines of our body, we expand outward into *samadhi*.

Samadhi (Bliss). This refers to an expansion of consciousness so complete that there is Self-realization, a state of union with everything in creation and, finally, with God beyond creation. Having merged with the light, we come to the realization that the whole of creation is made up of one light, and that our real nature is one of mystical union with that light, in everything and everyone.

Samadhi is an actual state of consciousness and not simply a mental idea or philosophy. It is much more than an imaginary condition or even just an expanded sense of compassion for others. Paramhansa Yogananda was one of the greatest yogis ever to live in the United States, and has been the inspiration for generations of meditators. He achieved the highest states of *samadhi*, and lived in that consciousness. Among other "miraculous" powers, he knew the thoughts of all of his students—not because he "read their minds," but because he was *in* them as much as he was in his own body. One time he remarked to a student, "You have a sour taste in your mouth." When the student expressed astonishment, he explained, "I am as much in your body as I am in mine." He often demonstrated his complete knowledge of the actions and thoughts of his disciples.

My teacher, Swami Kriyananda, spent several years with Yogananda and was trained by him personally. In Swami Kriyananda's wonderful book, *The Path—My Life with Paramhansa Yogananda*, he recounts a time when Yogananda was in the desert finishing his explanation of India's great scripture, the Bhagavad Gita.

In the evenings, Master exercised by walking slowly around his retreat compound. Generally he asked me to accompany him. He was so much withdrawn from body-consciousness on those occasions that he sometimes had to lean on my arm for support. He would pause and sway back and forth, as if about to fall.

"I am in so many bodies," Master remarked once, returning slowly to body-consciousness, "It is difficult for me to remember which body I am supposed to keep moving."

The attainment of *samadhi*, this highest state of consciousness, is the true goal of life. It is from this state that we, as the soul, descended into form. Within each of us burns the irrepressible yearning to return to our infinite origins. All outward fulfillments are but pale reflections of the bliss of *samadhi*.

Paramhansa Yogananda gave a wonderful account of this state in *Autobiography of a Yogi*. It takes place when his guru, Sri Yukteswar, deems him ready for this state of consciousness:

"He struck gently on my chest above the heart.

My body became immovably rooted; breath was drawn out of my lungs as if by some huge magnet. Soul and mind instantly lost their physical bondage, and streamed out like a fluid piercing light from my every pore. The flesh was as though dead, yet in my intense awareness I knew that never before had I been fully alive. My sense of identity was no longer narrowly confined to a body, but embraced the circumambient atoms. People on distant streets seemed to be moving gently over my own remote periphery. The roots of plants and trees appeared through a dim transparency of the soil; I discerned the inward flow of their sap.

The whole vicinity lay bare before me. My ordinary

frontal vision was now changed to a vast spherical sight, simultaneously all-perceptive. Through the back of my head I saw men strolling far down Rai Ghat Road, and noticed also a white cow who was leisurely approaching. When she reached the space in front of the open ashram gate, I observed her with my two physical eyes. As she passed by, behind the brick wall, I saw her clearly still.

All objects within my panoramic gaze trembled and vibrated like quick motion pictures. My body, Master's, the pillared courtyard, the furniture and floor, the trees and sunshine, occasionally became violently agitated, until all melted into a luminescent sea; even as sugar crystals, thrown into a glass of water, dissolve after being shaken. The unifying light alternated with materializations of form, the metamorphoses revealing the law of cause and effect in creation.

An oceanic joy broke upon calm endless shores of my soul. The Spirit of God, I realized, is exhaustless Bliss; His body is countless tissues of light. A swelling glory within me began to envelop towns, continents, the earth, solar and stellar systems, tenuous nebulae, and floating universes. The entire cosmos, gently luminous, like a city seen afar at night, glimmered within the infinitude of my being. The sharply etched global outlines faded somewhat at the farthest edges; there I could see a mellow radiance, ever-undiminished. It was indescribably subtle; the planetary pictures were formed of a grosser light.

The divine dispersion of rays poured from an Eternal Source, blazing into galaxies, transfigured with ineffable auras. Again and again I saw the creative beams condense into constellations, then resolve into sheets of transparent flame. By rhythmic reversion, sextillion worlds passed into diaphanous luster; fire became firmament.

I cognized the center of the empyrean as a point of intuitive perception in my heart. Irradiating splendor issued from my nucleus to every part of the universal structure. Blissful amrita, the nectar of immortality, pulsed through me with a quicksilverlike fluidity. The creative voice of God I heard resounding as Aum, the vibration of the Cosmic Motor. Suddenly the breath returned to my lungs. With a disappointment almost unbearable, I realized that my infinite immensity was lost. Once more I was limited to the humiliating cage of a body, not easily accommodative to the Spirit. Like a prodigal child, I had run away from my macrocosmic home and imprisoned myself in a narrow microcosm."

This state of total union is sought, consciously or unconsciously, by everyone. It is the ultimate goal of life. And yet each of us has the free will to seek the "ever new, ever expanding joy" of *samadhi*, or to turn, once again, toward the familiarity of old habits and attachments. The art and science of meditation beckons all those who choose to go toward the light.

While this book has introduced you to some of the most powerful techniques in yoga, nothing can be a substitute for actual practice. Two aids are especially important. First in importance is attuning your will with God. In order to be able to do this it is extremely helpful to have a teacher or *guru*.

Second in importance, according to the scriptures of India, is the company of other truth seekers. Seek out companions who will help and encourage you in your search for the Infinite.

Ananda has centers and meditation groups around the world where you can find guidance and encouragement. At one of our meditation retreats, The Expanding Light, located in Northern California, we offer classes in meditation and many other subjects. If you would like more information, please check our website **www.ananda.org**, or contact us at Ananda, 14618 Tyler Foote Road, Nevada City, California 95959.

May you, friend, be blessed through your practice of meditation with enlightenment—the true goal of all life. May God shower you with His grace, and may His light illumine your pathway home.

Afterword

The View from 40 Years of Teaching

I have taught and practiced this wonderful science for over 40 years, and have been able to observe the effects of meditation (especially the advanced technique of Kriya Yoga) on many of hundreds of friends and students. During most of that time I have lived in Ananda Village, a spiritual community based on meditation and the associated spiritual lifestyle. I also have been part of the staff of The Expanding Light, which is one of California's premier yoga and meditation retreats that serves over one thousand guests each year. All of this experience gives a broad base for observations about the value of meditation and allows a long-term perspective.

One of the things I've seen is that people benefit from meditation very quickly. Many guests report that within days of learning to meditate they have important, sometimes life-changing insights. Those who stay with their practice often feel that it is the single most beneficial thing they are doing for themselves.

A second important effect is that meditation is a catalyst for other important changes in behavior and attitude. People who meditate begin to look at how to improve other aspects of their lives. They tend to eat better, exercise more, and eliminate self-destructive habits like smoking and drinking. They also begin to introspect and eliminate harmful attitudes and behaviors.

While the benefits can be profound, meditation is not a magic pill. Meditation, like exercise, builds its power slowly but surely. Physiological and psychological changes need time to develop, especially if habits are deep seated. It takes commitment and effort to continue a daily practice, and those with false expectations can sometimes become discouraged. That said, meditation is extremely effective over the long run. Many people feel that meditation gives them back a part of themselves that has been missing. Most importantly, meditation begins to put us in touch with our own deepest nature and helps us find our authentic purpose. A life based on meditation is simply a happier way to live.

When a group of meditators live together, the power is amplified enormously. Ananda Village has some 250 members of all ages and races living a life based on spiritual principles. Seeing the harmony of life at Ananda, one gets a glimpse into a glorious future possibility for mankind. What happens when you have a life based on meditation, cooperation, healthy living, and mutual support? In over forty years at Ananda there has never been a truly violent act. Nor do we have a problem with crime, drugs, or prejudice—

things that are pandemic in society at large. This is not because the members are passive. In fact, they tend to be even more strong-willed than normal, having had to swim against the current to choose this kind of life. It is, rather, because meditation gives us the supreme tool to work on the root causes of conflict: those individual tendencies that protect the ego at the expense of others. I have experienced personally, and seen in others, the ability to go through some of life's deepest tests with equanimity and joy. The 40 years of experience at Ananda gives an abundance of proof that meditation can be the basis for a wonderful, happy life.

Paramhansa Yogananda's great book, *Autobiography of a Yogi*, ends with this sentiment: "Far into the night my dear friend—the first Kriya Yogi in America—discussed with me the need for world colonies founded on a spiritual basis. The ills attributed to an anthropomorphic abstraction called "society" may be laid more realistically at the door of Everyman. Utopia must spring in the private bosom before it can flower in civic virtue. Man is a soul, not an institution; his inner reforms alone can lend permanence to outer ones. By stress on spiritual values, self-realization, a colony exemplifying world brotherhood is empowered to send inspiring vibrations far beyond its locale."

I sincerely hope that you have experienced "inspiring vibrations" from this book. And I pray that the practice of meditation will bring joy into your life and light into the world.

INDEX

ABOUT THE AUTHOR

Jyotish Novak is a close friend and student of Swami Kriyananda, direct disciple of Paramhansa Yogananda. In 1968, Swami Kriyananda founded Ananda World-Brotherhood Village near Nevada City, California. Jyotish is a founding member of this yogic community, which is one of the most successful intentional communities in the world. He is also, along with his wife Devi, the Spiritual Director for Ananda Worldwide. As head of the Ananda Monastic Order, he offers spiritual guidance to hundreds of dedicated seekers in the various Ananda communities around the world. An inspiring teacher, he has spoken throughout the United States and Europe on spiritual subjects and yogic concepts. He is the author of several books on meditation and related subjects.

Jyotish and his wife live in Ananda World-Brotherhood Village.

Further Explorations

Other Offerings from Crystal Clarity

The *30-Day Essentials™* series

The *30-Day Essentials™* is a series of four-color, photographic gift books. Each book in the series is dedicated to giving inspirational, non-sectarian practices and advice to help readers enrich their life experiences.

30-Day Essentials for Marriage
Jyotish Novak

A step-by-step guide for establishing a new marriage, revitalizing an existing marriage, or enhancing an already solid one—all packaged in a beautiful, four-color gift book format, perfect for brides-to-be, newlyweds, or anniversaries. Featuring one inspiring piece of advice and one practical exercise per day, this book is a useful, light-hearted, and eye-catching way for couples to improve their relationship.

30-Day Essentials™ for Career
Jyotish Novak

    30-Day Essentials for Career is a beautiful, four-color gift book that features inspirational advice, quotations, and practical exercises for each of the qualities necessary for finding, building, and sustaining a successful career. Whether someone is looking for a new job, wanting to improve their current one, or simply wishing to clarify their career goals, *30-Day Essentials for Career* can help. Useful, light-hearted, and eye-catching, this book is the perfect tool for anyone who wants to improve their working life. Topics covered include: Harmony and Cooperation, Money Magnetism, Patience and Perseverance, Intuition and Decision Making, among many others.

DVD Titles by Jyotish Novak

Meditation Therapy™
Jyotish John Novak

Meditation Therapy™ is a bold, new approach to finding lasting solutions to our thorniest problems and concerns. Combining the insights of philosophy and psychology with the power of focused meditation practice, Meditation Therapy penetrates to the deepest levels of our being, helping us to change and improve ourselves at our very core. Each Meditation Therapy subject heading is divided into four parts: an introductory talk, a guided visualization, meditative stillness for intuitive solutions, and affirmations and other practical techniques. This DVD includes: Meditation Therapy for Relationships, Meditation Therapy for Stress and Change, Meditation Therapy for Health and Healing.

by Savitri Simpson

Chakras for Starters
Savitri Simpson

It is not easy to find a concise, easy-to-read guide to this most intriguing of topics, the chakras. In *Chakras for Starters*, Savitri Simpson demystifies and explains what chakras are, how to work with them, and the benefits accrued from doing so. Readers will learn how working with the chakras can help them feel a greater sense of security, self-control, heartfulness, centeredness, intuition, and spiritual transformation. Also available in MP3 audiobook format.

Praise for Chakras for Starters

"A well-conceived, practical, spiritual guide to the chakras, written with integrity and dedication. This is a beautiful work of heart and intelligence."
—Donna Eden, author of *Energy Medicine*, co-founder of *Innersource*

More DVDs from Ananda Yoga™

Ananda Yoga to Awaken the Chakras DVD

For people of all ages and levels of fitness, Yoga to Awaken the Chakras helps you work with the subtle energies of the body, leaving you feeling both calmed and rejuvenated. Beginning with a brief, easy-to-understand explanation of the chakras and the many benefits of working with them, this routine then moves into a step-by-step series of yoga postures designed to help you awaken and direct the energies of each chakra. You'll be guided through postures, mini-meditations, and deep relaxation that will help you develop an awareness of the chakras and their potential for self-transformation.

Bonus DVD Feature: A full-length talk by Savitri Simpson, author of *Chakras for Starters*, that provides a detailed, complete introduction to the chakras.

Books by Paramhansa Yogananda

Autobiography of a Yogi
Reprint of the Philosophical Library 1946 First Edition
Paramhansa Yogananda

This is a new edition, featuring previously unavailable material, of a true spiritual classic. *Autobiography of a Yogi* is one of the best-selling Eastern philosophy titles of all-time, with millions of copies sold, and named one of the best and most influential books of the 20th century. This highly prized verbatim reprinting of the original 1946 edition is the only one available free from textual changes made after Yogananda's death.

Yogananda was the first yoga master of India whose mission it was to live and teach in the West. His first-hand account of his life experiences includes childhood revelations, stories of his visits to saints and masters in India, and long-secret teachings of Self-realization that he made available to the Western reader.

This updated edition contains bonus materials, including a last chapter that Yogananda wrote in 1951, without posthumous changes. This edition also includes the eulogy that Yogananda wrote for Gandhi, and a new foreword and afterword by Swami Kriyananda, one of Yogananda's close, direct disciples.

Praise for Autobiography of a Yogi
"In the original edition, published during Yogananda's life, one is more in contact with Yogananda himself. While Yogananda founded centers and organizations, his concern was more with guiding individuals to direct communion with Divinity rather than with promoting any one church as

opposed to another. This spirit is easier to grasp in the original edition of this great spiritual and yogic classic."

—David Frawley, Director, American Institute of Vedic Studies, author of *Yoga: The Greater Tradition*

Autobiography of a Yogi Card Deck and Booklet
Paramhansa Yogananda

Each of the 52 cards features an inspiring quotation taken from the text of the original 1946 First Edition—the preferred edition for both enthusiasts and collectors. The flip side of each card features a photograph from the book or a previously unreleased and rare photograph of Yogananda. For the first time, these famous images and quotations will be portable, and can be used in your home, journal, auto, and purse. The enclosed booklet includes a history of the *Autobiography*, additional information about the quotations and photographs, and a user's guide for the card deck.

Books by Swami Kriyananda

The Path—My Life with Paramhansa Yogananda
One Man's Search on the Only Path There Is
Swami Kriyananda (J. Donald Walters)
What would it be like to live with a great spiritual master? Here, through over 400 stories and sayings of Paramhansa Yogananda, we learn more about the beloved author of *Autobiography of a Yogi*. Yogananda comes alive for us— his wisdom, compassion, divine love, sparkling sense of

humor, and respect for all. Through sharing the story of his own life with Yogananda, Kriyananda introduces the reader to the essence of the spiritual life and the attitudes necessary for living it successfully. If you loved *Autobiography of a Yogi*, you will love what many consider to be a companion volume. This is a vitally useful guide for sincere seekers on any path.

Praise for The Path

"Your openness, your undeviating devotion to a life of love and service, and your joyous good humor express themselves in your book. . . it came to an end too soon!"
—Ken Keyes, Jr., author of *Handbook to Higher Consciousness* and *Your Life is a Gift*

Affirmations for Self-Healing
Swami Kriyananda (J. Donald Walters)

We are what we think. Our thoughts about ourselves and life itself color everything that happens to us for good or ill. By consciously working with positive thoughts we can reprogram negative thought patterns in the subconscious. These 52 affirmations and prayers—one for each week of the year—will help you strengthen positive qualities in yourself such as good health, will power, forgiveness, security, happiness, and many others.

This inspirational book is the ultimate self-help manual—a powerful tool for personal transformation.

Praise for Affirmations for Self-Healing

"Kriyananda is a born, great teacher. His books are gentle masterpieces."
—Louise Hay, best-selling author of *You Can Heal Your Life*

"Swami Kriyananda is wise teacher whose words convey love and compassion. Read and listen, and allow your life to change."
— Larry Dossey, best-selling author of *Healing Words*

Ananda Yoga™ for Higher Awareness
Swami Kriyananda (J. Donald Walters)

This unique book teaches hatha yoga as it was originally intended: as a way to uplift your consciousness and aid your spiritual development. Kriyananda describes the classic poses clearly and simply, including photographs, and guides you in attuning to the power of each pose for awakening higher awareness, especially through the use of affirmations for each pose. Also includes suggestions for routines of varying lengths for both beginning and advanced students. Kriyananda is a world-renowned expert in yoga and meditation.

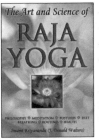

Ananda Course in Self-Realization, Parts 1 & 2
Lessons in Meditation and *The Art and Science of Raja Yoga*
Swami Kriyananda and *Jyotish Novak*

Part I: An excellent introduction to the basic techniques of meditation through clear, step-by-step instructions. This course introduces the techniques of the path of Kriya Yoga, including the Hong-Sau technique of concentration and Paramhansa Yogananda's Energization Exercises, a unique system for increasing your energy level and overcoming fatigue. There are also simple suggestions on how to sit comfortably for meditation, how to still the restless mind, and how to take experiences of peace and joy into daily life. Includes an illustrated, lay-flat book and two CDs with guided meditations, visualizations, and guided Energization Exercises.

Part II: The Art and Science of Raja Yoga is more than a book—it is a fascinating resource you will review again and again throughout your life as you explore the path of yoga. The course develops through seven major topics—Philosophy, Meditation, Postures, Breathing, Routines, Healing Principles and Techniques, and Diet. The author, Swami Kriyananda, a world-renowned expert on the science and art of yoga, brings the depth yoga to life for you with all its thrilling clarity and insight. You'll find these teachings practical, enjoyable to read, and easy to apply in your own life.

Comes with a CD, which includes a talk: "Meditation: The Great Problem Solver"; a 40-minute Ananda Yoga for Higher Awareness session; and a guided visualization, "Guided Meditation On The Light."

Energization Exercises set

The Energization Exercises, as taught in the Ananda Course in Self-Realization, are a wonderful system of exercises originated by Paramhansa Yogananda. They are, undoubtedly, his unique contribution to the science of yoga.

This set includes: a beautiful, glossy-finished 22x17-inch poster with figures showing each of the 39 Energization Exercises, an excellent, quick reference for how to do each exercise properly and in the correct order; a DVD with Barbara Bingham and Swami Kriyananda performing the exercises; a CD with a guided explanation of the exercises; and a booklet with illustrations and explanations of the exercises.

Music and Audiobooks from Clarity Sound & Light

Bliss Chants CD
By Ananda Kirtan

Chanting focuses and lifts the mind to higher states of consciousness. *Bliss Chants* features chants written by Yogananda and his direct disciple Swami Kriyananda. They're performed by Ananda Kirtan, a group of singers and musicians from Ananda, one of the world's most respected yoga communities. Chanting is accompanied by guitar, harmonium, kirtals, and tabla.

Praise for Bliss Chants

"The combined voices of Ananda Kirtan provide bliss indeed! These singers chant the sacred poetry of Paramhansa Yogananda and Swami Kriyananda, including pieces like 'O God Beautiful' and 'I Will Drink Thy Name.' The music has a strong sense of happiness and joy. Even in CD form, it's easy to sense the camaraderie in the room and one can easily imagine the singers swaying and smiling as they sing. Besides voice, the album also features catchy rhythms, harmonium in the backdrop and guitar."
—Music Design

Divine Mother Chants CD
By Ananda Kirtan

Chanting helps open the heart to God, an important aid to deep meditation. The chants on this recording, written by Paramhansa Yogananda and his direct disciple Swami Kriyananda, will help you experience the feminine and loving aspect of the Divine. Chanting is accompanied by guitar, harmonium, kirtals, and tabla.

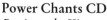 **Power Chants CD**
By Ananda Kirtan

These particular chants of Paramhansa Yogananda and his direct disciple Swami Kriyananda will help you tap into the positive aspects of Power: the ability to strengthen and direct our will, creative energy, and inner resources toward the Divine, and to use our Power to control our spiritual destiny. Chanting is accompanied by guitar, harmonium, kirtals, and tabla.

Metaphysical Meditation CD
Guided Visualizations Based on the Poetry of Paramhansa Yogananda
Swami Kriyananda

These thirteen guided meditations, based on the mystical poetry of Paramhansa Yogananda, are ideal for evoking deep, spiritual awareness. Set to a background of well-known and inspiring classical music, *Metaphysical Meditations* draws listeners inward to the calm, joyful, expansive states of awareness that accompany deep meditation. Ideal for both beginning and experienced meditators, this is one of our most popular products and has been completely redesigned and re-mastered.

CRYSTAL CLARITY PUBLISHERS

When you're seeking a book on practical spiritual living, you want to know it's based on an authentic tradition of timeless teachings and resonates with integrity.

This is our goal: to offer you books of practical wisdom filled with true spiritual principles that have not only been tested through the ages but also through personal experience.

Started in 1968, Crystal Clarity is the publishing house of Ananda, a spiritual community dedicated to meditation and living by true values, as shared by Paramhansa Yogananda, and his direct disciple, Swami Kriyananda, the founder of Ananda. The members of our staff and each of our authors live by these principles. Our worldwide work touches thousands whose lives have been enriched by these universal teachings.

We publish only books that combine creative thinking, universal principles, and a timeless message. Crystal Clarity books will open doors to help you discover more fulfillment and joy by living and acting from the center of peace within you.

Recognized worldwide for its bestselling, original, unaltered edition of Paramhansa Yogananda's classic *Autobiography of a Yogi*, Crystal Clarity offers many additional resources to assist you in your spiritual journey, including over ninety books, a wide variety of inspirational and relaxation music composed by Swami Kriyananda, Yogananda's direct disciple, and yoga and meditation DVDs.

To request a catalog, place an order for the products you read about in the Further Explorations section of this book, or to find out more information about us and our products, please contact us:

Crystal Clarity Publishers   clarity@crystalclarity.com
14618 Tyler Foote Road   800.424.1055 / 530.478.7600
Nevada City, CA 95959   fax: 530.478.7610

For our online catalog, complete with secure ordering, please visit us on the web at: **www.crystalclarity.com.**

Crystal Clarity Publishers' music and audiobooks are available on all the popular online download services. Look for us in your favorite online music catalog.

Ananda Worldwide

Swami Kriyananda lived with his guru during the last four years of the Master's life, and continued to serve his organization for another ten years, bringing the teachings of Kriya Yoga and Self-realization to audiences in the United States, Europe, Australia, and, from 1958–1962, India. In 1968, together with a small group of close friends and students, he founded the first "world brotherhood community" in the foothills of the Sierra Nevada Mountains in northeastern California. Initially a meditation retreat center located on 67 acres of forested land, Ananda World-Brotherhood Community today encompasses 1,000 acres where about 250 people live a dynamic, fulfilling life based on the principles and practices of spiritual, mental, and physical development, cooperation, respect, and divine friendship.

At this writing, after forty years of existence, Ananda is one of the most successful networks of intentional communities in the world. Urban communities have been developed in Sacramento and Palo Alto (CA), Seattle (WA), Portland (OR), as well as a retreat center and European community in Assisi, Italy and a center and community near New Delhi, India. The Expanding Light, a guest retreat for spiritual studies visited by over 2,000 people each year, offers courses in Self-realization and related subjects.

Ananda Sangha Contact Information

mail: 14618 Tyler Foote Road
Nevada City, CA 95959

phone: 530.478.7560

online: www.ananda.org

email: sanghainfo@ananda.org

Ananda's guest retreat, The Expanding Light, offers a varied, year round schedule of classes and workshops on yoga, meditation, and spiritual practice. You may also come for a relaxed personal renewal, participating in ongoing activities as much or as little as you wish.

The beautiful serene mountain setting, supportive staff, and delicious vegetarian food provide an ideal environment for a truly meaningful, spiritual vacation.

Expanding Light Contact Information

phone: 800.346.5350

online: www.expandinglight.org

email: info@expandinglight.org